MATH GIRLS

TALK ABOUT

EQUATIONS & GRAPHS

Fundamental Skills for Advanced Mathematics

BY HIROSHI YUKI

Author of MATH GIRLS

(x, y)

$y = \frac{a}{x}$

TRANSLATED BY TONY GONZALEZ

MATH GIRLS TALK ABOUT EQUATIONS AND GRAPHS

Originally published as *Suugaku Gaaru No Himitsu Nooto Shiki To Gurafu*
Copyright © 2013 Hiroshi Yuki
Softbank Creative Corp., Tokyo

English translation © 2014 by Tony Gonzalez
Edited by Joseph Reeder
Additional editing by Alexander O. Smith
Cover design by Kasia Bytnerowicz

Published 2014 by

Bento Books, Inc.
Austin, Texas 78732

bentobooks.com

ISBN 978-1-939326-22-5 (hardcover)
ISBN 978-1-939326-19-5 (trade paperback)
Library of Congress Control Number: 2014936458

Printed in the United States of America
First edition, May 2014

Math Girls Talk About
Equations and Graphs

To My Readers

This book is a collection of conversations between Miruka, Tetra, Yuri, and our narrator.

If there are places where you don't understand what they're talking about, or equations you don't understand, feel free to skip over those parts. But please do your best to keep up with them.

That's the best way to make yourself part of the conversation.

—Hiroshi Yuki

Cast of Characters

I am your narrator. I'm a junior in high school, and I love math. Equations in particular.

Miruka is my age. She's so good at math, it's scary. She has long black hair and wears metal frame glasses.

Tetra is one year younger than me, and a bundle of energy. She cuts her hair short and has big, beautiful eyes.

Yuri is my cousin, an eighth grader. She has a chestnut ponytail and excels at logic.

Ms. Mizutani is our school librarian.

Mom is, well, just my mom.

Contents

Prologue

Conversations contain everything. Doubts and answers, agreement and arguments, praise and criticism. Space. Time. And secrets.

We share our secrets through conversation. We share the secrets hidden in equations and graphs. Secrets hidden in identities and simultaneous equations. In parabolas and hyperbolic curves.

Math isn't about whether you can solve a given problem. It's about tackling things head on and thinking deeply. It's about asking questions and finding answers.

The conversations we have together become our new secrets, replacing the secrets they helped us uncover. Precious secrets that no one else will ever know, and no one can ever steal.

These are our conversations.

CHAPTER 1

Letters and Identities

"Time to become a problem solver."

1.1 BUGGED BY LETTERS

Tetra   "There you are!"

Me   "Hey, Tetra. Looks like something's got you psyched."

Tetra   "You know me."

Me   "But this *is* the library. Maybe we should keep it down a bit?"

Tetra   "Oh, right."

Tetra was by far the giddiest of my friends. She was in tenth grade, one year behind me. She cut her hair short and had big, beautiful eyes. We met in the library after school almost every day, where we talked about all kinds of things. Well, all kinds of mathy things, at least.

Tetra   "Okay to ask you about something?"

Me   "Of course. What is it?"

Tetra sits down next to me.

Tetra   "When I study math, I always get confused about when to use what letters. I look at the equations in my book and wonder, 'Why did they use these letters? Why didn't they use something else?'"

Me   "Give me an example."

Tetra   "An example?"

Me   "Sure. Show me an equation where the letters bug you."

Tetra   "Hard to do off the top of my head."

Me   "Well then just give me any equation, and let's talk about the letters in it."

Tetra   "Okay, let's see..."

Tetra looks up while she thinks.

Tetra   "How about this one?"

$$(a + b)(a - b) = a^2 - b^2$$

Tetra   "That's how my teacher wrote it on the board. But in my book, it looks like this."

$$(x + y)(x - y) = x^2 - y^2$$

Me   "That's an example of an identity."

Tetra   "A whatity?"

Me   "An identity. An equation that will always be true, no matter what numbers you stick into it. This equation $(a+b)(a-b) = a^2 - b^2$ always holds, no matter what a and b are, so it's an identity. If you want to be precise, it's an identity on a and b."

Tetra   "Gotcha!"

Me   "This is a good one to remember, by the way. Just think, 'the product of a sum and a difference is a difference of squares.' So when you have a sum $a+b$ and a difference $a-b$, if you multiply those two together you'll get a^2-b^2. Since that's an identity, it's always true, no matter what values a and b have."

Tetra   "Well what about $(x+y)(x-y)=x^2-y^2$?"

Me   "Same thing. This one is an identity on x and y, so that's a true statement, no matter what x and y are."

Tetra   "So which one is right, a and b, or x and y? When do I use one or the other?"

Me   "In this case, it doesn't really matter."

$$(a+b)(a-b)=a^2-b^2 \quad \text{an identity on } a \text{ and } b$$
$$(x+y)(x-y)=x^2-y^2 \quad \text{an identity on } x \text{ and } y$$

Tetra   "So I've been worrying all this time about something that doesn't matter?"

         Tetra crosses her arms.

Me   "This thing about the letters really *does* bug you, doesn't it."

Tetra   "Yeah. I think my problems with math began when these letters started popping up. Now it's a, b, c this and x, y, z that. I even see Greek letters sometimes!"

Me   "I hadn't really thought about it, but you're right. After a point, math is more about letters than numbers."

Tetra   "Maybe I'm just being silly. I'm slow enough as it is without worrying about this kind of thing."

Me   "You aren't slow, you're careful. There's a big difference. But the important thing isn't which letters are being *used*, it's what they *mean*. That's what you really need to pay attention to."

Tetra   "What do you mean, what they mean?"

Me   "Math is something you have to read carefully, not skim through. You need to go slow, and pay attention to what those letters are doing, and why they're there."

1.2 Where Do the Letters Reappear?

Me   "Another thing to keep an eye out for is where letters reappear."

Tetra   "I never knew they *dis*appeared."

Me   "That's not what I mean. Here, check out this identity we were talking about."

$$(a + b)(a - b) = a^2 - b^2$$

Me   "See how the a and b show up in several places? One of the rules of math is that when a letter is repeated, it has to mean the same thing. So the a in the $(a + b)(a - b)$ on the left side of this equation and the a in the $a^2 - b^2$ on the right have to represent the same number."

Tetra   "Wait, you lost me. You're saying that a is always the same number?"

Me   "Not quite. I'm saying it's always the same number in *this* equation. As long as we're talking about the identity $(a + b)(a - b) = a^2 - b^2$, every a has to represent the same number, and so does every b. Of course a and b might represent the same number too."

Tetra   "Okay, I see what you're saying, but—"

Me   "But why am I reviewing something you learned years ago?"

Tetra   "Something like that, yeah."

Me	"Because I want to show you how something cool happens when you plug numbers into those a's and b's. Let's start with $a = 100, b = 2$. That means we're substituting a 100 for all the a's and a 2 for all the b's."

| Tetra | "How do you know those are right answers?" |

| Me | "Because this is an identity, remember? That means it works for *any* numbers we pick." |

| Tetra | "Oh, of course." |

| Me | "Here's what we get after substituting." |

$(a + b)(a - b) = a^2 - b^2$ "product of a sum and a difference"
$(\underline{100} + b)(\underline{100} - b) = \underline{100}^2 - b^2$ substitute a's with 100 as an example
$(100 + \underline{2})(100 - \underline{2}) = 100^2 - \underline{2}^2$ substitute b's with 2 as an example
$\underline{102} \times \underline{98} = 100^2 - 2^2$ calculate the left side
$102 \times 98 = \underline{10000} - \underline{4}$ calculate the right side

| Tetra | "Okay, so?" |

| Me | "So we found this equation." |

$$102 \times 98 = 10000 - 4$$

| Tetra | "Sorry, I still don't see where this is headed." |

Tetra gives a doubtful frown.

1.3 MENTAL ARITHMETIC

| Me | "Let's start with the left side of that equation." |

$$\underbrace{102 \times 98}_{\text{left side}} = 10000 - 4$$

| Me | "Calculating 102×98 in your head is kinda tough, right?" |

Tetra   "Yeah, wow. Let's see, 8 × 2 is—"

Me   "No, you don't have to do all that. Look at the right side of the equation."

$$102 \times 98 = \underbrace{10000 - 4}_{\text{right side}}$$

Me   "It's just $10000 - 4$. Much easier."

Tetra   "Sure, 9996, right?"

Me   "See how we've turned something hard like 102×98 into a simple subtraction problem?"

Tetra   "I think so."

Me   "The trick is looking at 102×98, and noticing that 102 is $100 + 2$, and that 98 is $100 - 2$. Once you start playing around and plugging actual numbers into an identity like $(a + b)(a - b) = a^2 - b^2$, you'll get the hang of it in no time. Half the things they teach you in those mental arithmetic books rely on identities like this. Kinda fun, really."

Miruka   "What's kinda fun?"

Miruka appears out of nowhere, and I nearly fall out of my seat.

Tetra   "Miruka, stop sneaking up on us like that!"

Me   "At least make some sound when you walk."

Miruka   "Yeah, yeah. So tell me, what's fun?"

Miruka was a classmate. She had long, black hair and wore metal frame glasses. When it came to math, she had us all beat—but it was more than that. Miruka had this certain poise that made it hard for me to tear my eyes away from her.

Miruka peers at the notebook I've been writing in.

Miruka   " 'The product of a sum and a difference is a difference of squares.' Hmph."

Tetra   "We were studying identities."

$$(a + b)(a - b) = a^2 - b^2$$

Miruka   "About how this identity changes rectangles into squares?"

Tetra   "Uh, not exactly."

Miruka   "Here, take a look."

Miruka sketches a quick graph.

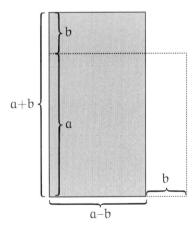

$(a + b)(a - b)$ as a rectangle

Me   "Oh, I get it!"

Tetra   "I don't. What's this a graph of?"

Me	"A rectangle where the length of one side is $a + b$, and the other is $a - b$. So its area is the product of the two, $(a + b)(a - b)$! Of course!"
Miruka	"And this one is a figure for $a^2 - b^2$. You can make it using the two squares."

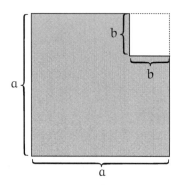

$a^2 - b^2$ as two squares

Tetra	"Two squares? Where did they come from?"
Me	"You start with a big square with area a^2, then chop out a square corner that has an area of b^2."
Miruka	"Precisely."

Miruka's eyes gleam.

Tetra	"Oh! You just moved the smaller rectangle down and to the right. And just moving it doesn't change the area!"

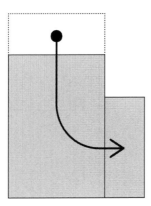

Me   "This shows you exactly what's going on in the equation $(a + b)(a - b) = a^2 - b^2$. The $(a + b)(a - b)$ on the left is the area of the big rectangle. The $a^2 - b^2$ on the right is the area of the big square with the area of the little square taken out."

Tetra   "Makes perfect sense!"

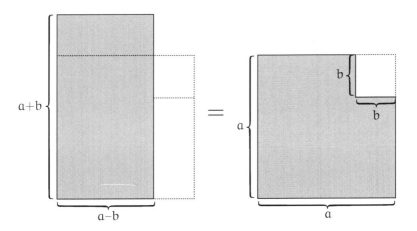

A graphical representation of $(a + b)(a - b) = a^2 - b^2$

| Me | "This also explains why $(a + b)(a - b) = a^2 - b^2$ is an identity." |

Miruka cocks her head.

Miruka	"Well, don't get too carried away. This geometric explanation only works if a and b are real numbers, and greater than zero."
Tetra	"So you can't do this all the time?"
Miruka	"Yes and no. The identity $(a + b)(a - b) = a^2 - b^2$ is supposed to be true for *any* values of a and b. But there are some assumptions built into this graph, namely that $a \geqslant 0$ and $b \geqslant 0$. Do you see why?"
Tetra	"Because we're talking about side lengths, and those can't be negative?"
Me	"That's right. Actually there's another assumption in this graph, that $a > b$. A picture's worth a thousand words, but they can make it easy to overlook the conditions that come with them. Score one for equations."
Tetra	"Is this what you meant when you were talking about the meaning behind the letters?"
Me	"Exactly. Good eye!"
Miruka	"What's all this about?"
Me	"Just before you snuck up on us, I was telling Tetra how it's important to be sure you understand what the letters in equations stand for."
Miruka	"So that's the kind of thing you two talk about."
Tetra	"He was also showing me how to stick numbers into $(a + b)(a-b) = a^2-b^2$ to do tricky calculations like 102×98."

$$(a + b)(a - b) = a^2 - b^2 \quad \text{"product of a sum and a difference"}$$
$$(100 + 2)(100 - 2) = 100^2 - 2^2 \quad \text{substitute } a = 100, b = 2$$
$$102 \times 98 = 10000 - 4 \quad \text{calculate } 102 \times 98 \text{ as } 10000 - 4$$

Tetra   "Now I can do 102×98 in my head!"

1.4 Expanding Expressions

Me   "Don't worry, Tetra. I think a lot of people get lost when letters start creeping into math. The way they teach us doesn't help."

Tetra   "It is a little confusing. In class we move stuff around to solve for x or whatever, but I have no idea what's going on. It drives me nuts."

Me   "Your teacher's just getting you to practice before you start on cooler stuff."

Miruka   "I thought you loved messing with equations."

Me   "I do. Especially expanding things out and factorizations. I liked it so much in junior high I spent hours in the library after school doing more of it. After a while, it all starts to come naturally. Good old $(a + b)(a - b)$ and I spent many an afternoon chasing after $a^2 - b^2$."

$$
\begin{aligned}
&(a + b)(a - b) \\
&= \underline{(a + b)}a - \underline{(a + b)}b && \text{distribute the } (a + b) \\
&= \underline{aa + ba} - (a + b)b && \text{expand the } (a + b)a \text{ part} \\
&= aa + ba - \underline{(ab + bb)} && \text{expand the } (a + b)b \text{ part} \\
&= aa + ba \underline{\;- ab - bb} && \text{get rid of the parentheses} \\
&= aa + \underline{ab} - ab - bb && \text{rewrite } ba \text{ as } ab \\
&= aa - bb && ab - ab \text{ is 0, so it goes away} \\
&= \underline{a^2} - bb && \text{rewrite } aa \text{ as } a^2 \\
&= a^2 - \underline{b^2} && \text{rewrite } bb \text{ as } b^2
\end{aligned}
$$

Me   "That's the equations-only way of getting from $(a + b)(a - b)$ to $a^2 - b^2$. We're just moving things around, so this should work for any values a and b. No worries about hidden conditions like with figures, either. Work that out yourself a few times, and you'll never forget the identity."

Tetra   "Erm, if you say so."

Me   "Something wrong?"

Tetra   "No, nothing. I guess I get how playing with identities can be fun. It's all about learning new tricks for calculating stuff, right? And looking at things using graphs like Miruka did is kinda neat."

Me   "I think so, at least."

Tetra   "I guess I just have to try harder to—"

Ms. Mizutani "The library is *closed!*"

Ms. Mizutani was our school librarian. She always wore a drum-tight skirt and glasses so dark they looked like sunglasses. Every day when it was time to lock up, she marched to the center of the room and announced that the library was closed. This wasn't the first time her proclamation had cut short one of our math talks.

"Skillful problem solvers must also be skillful readers."

Problems for Chapter 1

Problem 1-1 (Expanding expressions)

Expand the following:

$$(x + y)^2$$

(Answer on page 131)

Problem 1-2 (Calculating expressions)

Letting x be 3 and y be -2, calculate the following:

$$x^2 + 2xy + y^2$$

(Answer on page 132)

Problem 1-3 (Products of sums and differences)

Calculate the following:

$$202 \times 198$$

(Answer on page 133)

CHAPTER 2

The Appeal of Simultaneous Equations

"Problem solvers take problems to
other realms . . ."

2.1 HARD TO PUT INTO WORDS

I never liked words. I wasn't good with them. It was hard for me to put my feelings into words and deliver them as a message, and when I did finally spit something out, it was hard to be sure I hadn't been misunderstood.

Though to be honest, it wasn't so much that it was hard—it was that I was afraid. Not afraid that I'd be misunderstood, but afraid that someone might understand me. I didn't want anyone to see how small and ridiculous I was. So I kept my mouth shut.

These were the sort of thoughts going through my head one Saturday afternoon when Yuri dropped in.

2.2 YURI'S HOMEWORK

Yuri   "Hey, cuz! Whatcha doin'?"

Me   "Studying, as you can see."

Yuri   "Ugh, math again. You are *such* a nerd."

My cousin Yuri was in eighth grade. She lived just up the street, and she treated my house like an extension of her own. She had a chestnut-brown ponytail.

Me   "You're just jealous. What's that you brought?"

Yuri   "My notebook and a worksheet. I came by to do home-work."

          Yuri slides on her glasses and spreads her work out on our living room table.

Me   "Make yourself at home."

Yuri   "Just be glad I'm taking this stuff seriously now."

Me   "Of course I'm—ooh, simultaneous equations!"

Yuri   "Quiet. Girl at work here."

Problem

Solve the following system of equations:

$$\begin{cases} x + y = 5 \\ 2x + 4y = 16 \end{cases}$$

Me   "Oh, that's an easy one. You just—"

Yuri   "Is your jawbone incapable of disengaging?"

Me   "Sorry, sorry. Sheesh."

          Yuri scribbles in her notebook for a few moments and then looks up.

Yuri   "That wasn't so bad."

Me   "Here, lemme see. Wow, what a mess."

$$2x + 2y = 10$$
$$2x + 4y = 16$$
$$2y = 6$$
$$y = 3$$
$$2x + 6 = 10$$
$$x = 2$$

Yuri   "It's right though, isn't it? Piece of cake."

Me   "You haven't even shown what the answer is."

Yuri   "Sure I did. Here and here. $y = 3$ and $x = 2$."

Me   "Well you got the right values, but everything's all jumbled up."

Yuri   "Don't be so picky. If the numbers are right, that's good enough."

           Yuri nods sagely.

2.3 MATH IS COMMUNICATION

Me   "Yuri, your answers are a message. If your answer's a mess, your message won't get across."

Yuri   "But I got the right answer!"

Me   "I'm not saying you didn't."

Yuri   "What *are* you trying to say then?"

Me   "That if you're lucky, your teacher will find your correct answer in this jumble, but you're betting that they're going to try that hard. You sure you want to make that bet?"

Yuri	"So what should I do?"
Me	"Remember that you're communicating. You need to show how you thought the problem out, how you solved it, and what your answer is. Your math needs a bit more appeal."
Yuri	"Just tell me how I should do it."
Me	"For starters, be more organized in how you write everything out. Start by writing the system of equations."
Yuri	"Okay, done."

$$x + y = 5$$
$$2x + 4y = 16$$

| Me | "You still aren't showing that this is a system of equations. Here, I'm gonna write down some rules for you to follow to make all this clearer." |

Writing systems of equations

- Use a curly bracket ({) on the left to indicate a system of equations.

- Align equals signs to tidy things up.

- Number equations to make your solution more clear.

| Yuri | "Fine, we'll write it your way." |

$$\begin{cases} x + y & = 5 & \cdots \text{①} \\ 2x + 4y & = 16 & \cdots \text{②} \end{cases}$$

| Me | "Good. Now what's the first thing you did to solve this?" |

Yuri   "I doubled and subtracted."

Me   "To be more specific, you doubled ① and subtracted like terms from ② to get rid of the 2x. Like this."

$$
\begin{array}{rll}
2x + 4y =\ & 16 & \cdots \text{equation } ② \\
- (2x + 2y =\ & 10) & \cdots \text{subtract } ① \times 2 \\
\hline
2y =\ & 6 &
\end{array}
$$

Yuri   "That's what I said."

Me   "So just write it out. Use some simple way to show what you're doubling, and what's being subtracted from what. You doubled both sides of ①, then subtracted the result from ②, right? You can write that out in words, or as an expression, like $② - ① \times 2$."

Yuri   "Okay, sure."

Me   "To be really detailed I guess you should say something like, 'Obtain $2y = 6$ from calculating $② - ① \times 2$,' but in an answer to a problem I guess we can abbreviate a bit."

$$
\begin{cases}
x + y\ \ = 5 & \cdots ① \\
2x + 4y = 16 & \cdots ②
\end{cases}
$$

from $② - ① \times 2$

$$2y = 6$$

Me   "So what did you do next?"

Yuri   "The $2y = 6$ part. I divided by 2."

Me   "Divided both sides of the equation by 2, right?"

$$\vdots$$

$$2y = 6$$

divide both sides by 2

$$y = 3$$

Yuri   "That means x has to be 2, since $x + y = 5$ and y is 3."

Me   "That's right, but to write that out you have to say something about substituting $y = 3$ in ①. We gave those things names to make writing out stuff like this simpler, so we might as well use them."

$$\vdots$$

substitute $y = 3$ in ①

$$x + 3 = 5$$
$$x = 2$$

Yuri   "See? Told you I got it right. y is 3 and x is 2."

Answer: $y = 3, \quad x = 2$

Me   "The problem isn't your answer, it's how you're answering. Even your answer here can be improved; you should write things in order, with the x before the y. When you write it backwards, you're making the reader stop and sort things out."

Yuri   "Fair enough."

Answer: $x = 2, \quad y = 3$

Me   "So to sum everything up, here's how I would answer this problem."

Answer

Solve the following system of equations:

$$\begin{cases} x + y = 5 & \cdots \text{①} \\ 2x + 4y = 16 & \cdots \text{②} \end{cases}$$

Answer

from ② − ① × 2

$$2y = 6$$

divide both sides by 2

$$y = 3$$

substitute $y = 3$ in ①

$$x + 3 = 5$$
$$x = 2$$

Answer: $x = 2, \quad y = 3$

Yuri   "You write your answers like that every time? Be honest!"

Me   "Well...no. But it's important to be able to."

Yuri   "Like I said: too much work."

Me   "You don't *always* have to write in so much detail."

Yuri   "So when do I?"

Me   "Read the problem. It says, 'Solve the following system of equations,' right? An answer like this makes it clear that you know how to do that. It shows that you read the problem carefully, too."

Yuri   "So when can I cut corners?"

Me   "When you're working on a bigger problem, and this was just one step along the way."

Yuri   "What's that supposed to mean?"

Me   "When you start working on more advanced stuff, sometimes solving a system of equations will be just one step toward your answer. If that's the case, you might even just write something like 'solving the system of equations gives $x = 2$, $y = 3$,' because that solution isn't the big message you're trying to get across to the reader. But in the case of homework, that's not the message you want to send to your teacher."

Yuri   "I thought all I had to do was get the right answer."

Me   "The answer is important, sure. But *how* you answer counts, too. An answer that includes every step you took not only shows that you really know what you're doing, it also helps *you* be sure you've done everything right."

Yuri takes off her glasses and smirks.

Me   "What?"

Yuri   "You. You always get so heated up over math."

Me   "Ha ha, very funny."

I take another glance at the solution.

Me   "Hang on, I just noticed something about this problem."

Yuri   "What?"

$$\begin{cases} x + y & = 5 & \cdots \text{①} \\ 2x + 4y & = 16 & \cdots \text{②} \end{cases}$$

Me   "The ② line here, $2x + 4y = 16$. Everything's divisible by 2."

$$2x + 4y = 16$$
$$\downarrow \text{ divide both sides by 2}$$
$$x + 2y = 8$$

Yuri   "Hey, yeah."

Me   "That makes for a much simpler solution."

Alternate Answer

Solve the following system of equations:

$$\begin{cases} x + y & = 5 & \cdots ① \\ 2x + 4y & = 16 & \cdots ② \end{cases}$$

Answer

divide both sides of ② by 2

$$x + 2y = 8 \qquad \cdots ③$$

from ③ − ①

$$y = 3$$

substitute $y = 3$ in ①

$$x + 3 = 5$$
$$x = 2$$

<u>Answer: $x = 2$ $y = 3$</u>

Yuri   "This is simpler? Looks about the same to me."

Me   "Lemme see that worksheet."

Yuri   "What, this?"

Me   "Just as I thought. A leg-counting problem."

Yuri   "A . . . what?"

2.4 COUNTING LEGS

Me   "A leg-counting problem. Cranes and turtles, in this case.
           It says so right here."

Problem (Counting legs)

- There are a total of 5 cranes and turtles.

- There are 16 legs among them.

- How many cranes and how many turtles are there?

Me   "These are fun."

Yuri   "There is *nothing* fun about word problems."

Me   "But you've already done all the work! You solved the
           system of equations, so just look at the problem like
           this."

- There are x cranes.

- There are y turtles.

- The total number of cranes and turtles is 5, so $x + y = 5$.

Me   "All we've done here is rewrite the line about the number
           of cranes and turtles as an equation."

          I point at Yuri's worksheet.

Yuri   "Yup."

Me   "Now we just need one more equation, one for this line
            about the total number of legs."

- Cranes have two legs, so if there are x cranes there must be 2x
  crane legs.

- Turtles have four legs, so if there are y turtles there must be
  4y turtle legs.

- Since there are 16 legs in all, $2x + 4y = 16$.

Me   "Together, these make up the system of equations we
            were working on."

$$\begin{cases} x + y & = 5 \\ 2x + 4y & = 16 \end{cases}$$

Yuri   "Yup."

Me   "By creating the system of equations, we've taken this
            problem about cranes and turtles into the world of
            math."

Answer (Counting legs)

- There are a total of 5 cranes and turtles.

- There are 16 legs among them.

- How many cranes and how many turtles are there?

Answer

- Create the first equation regarding the number of cranes and turtles.

  ▷ There are x cranes.

  ▷ There are y turtles.

  ▷ There are 5 cranes and turtles in all, so $x+y = 5$.

- Create the second equation regarding the number of legs.

  ▷ Cranes have 2 legs, so there are $2x$ crane legs in all.

  ▷ Turtles have 4 legs, so there are $4y$ turtle legs in all.

  ▷ There are 16 legs in all, so $2x + 4y = 16$.

From the above, we obtain the following system of equations:

$$\begin{cases} x + y & = 5 \\ 2x + 4y & = 16 \end{cases}$$

Solving this, we obtain $x = 2$, $y = 3$. Therefore, there are two cranes and three turtles.

Answer: 2 cranes, 3 turtles

Yuri	"Yup."
Me	"What's with all the 'yup's?"
Yuri	"Because this stuff is obvious. And boring. And too much work."

Yuri swishes her ponytail.

2.5 THINKING HARD

Me	"How can it be too much work, when I did all the work for you?"
Yuri	"I'm getting tired just watching. Problems like this aren't worth all that effort. All you have to do is think it through. You don't have to waste time writing down all these equations and systems and stuff."
Me	"How so?"
Yuri	"Because you know there's going to be a whole number of cranes and turtles. You just have to think about how many of each."
Me	"By 'whole number,' you mean 'integer,' right?"
Yuri	"Which ones were those again?"
Me	"Numbers like $\ldots -3, -2, -1, 0, 1, 2, 3 \ldots$?"
Yuri	"Yeah, those ones."
Me	"You sure? I've never heard of a negative turtle."
Yuri	"Ugh! You know what I mean! Since you know the answers are one of those, you just think it out: '5 animals with 16 legs? Uhh...2 and 3!' Like that."
Me	"What's going on in your head during the 'Uhh...' part?"

Yuri   "Well, just start with five cranes. That would mean ten legs, right?"

5 cranes have 10 legs

Me   "Yeah, sure. Five cranes, two legs each, $5 \times 2 = 10$. Go on."

Yuri   "We want 16 legs, so you can't do it with just cranes. Gotta add some turtles. Replace one crane with a turtle, and you get twelve legs, right?"

4 cranes and 1 turtle have 12 legs

Me   "So now we're up to twelve legs."

Yuri   "Wash, rinse, repeat until you get sixteen legs."

3 cranes and 2 turtles have 14 legs

2 cranes and 3 turtles have 16 legs

Yuri   "See? We got sixteen legs without messing around with systems of equations and all that. It's called *brain power*."

Me   "Okay, I'll admit that a system of equations is overkill for this particular problem."

Yuri   "No duh."

Me   "But learning how to count reptiles and waterfowl isn't the point. You're learning how to use math to solve problems."

2.6 WHY WE USE MATH

Me   "Sure, you can think your way through it if you just want to count a few animal legs. But what you're *really* learning is how to tackle problems that are too complex to work out by just thinking. You're learning things like how to represent unknowns as a variable, and how to express the relation between unknowns as an equation."

Yuri   "That's deep."

Me   "It sorta is. If you think about it, saying 'there are x cranes' is an amazingly powerful statement. The problem doesn't tell you how many cranes there are, but this sentence lets you manipulate the number of cranes anyway. You just let that unknown hang around as a letter."

Yuri   "And the turtles are hanging around in y, I guess."

Me   "Yup. Makes it easier later on if we assign letters to these unknowns, rather than just make them all question marks or something."

Yuri   "Less thought involved with the question marks."

Me   "Couldn't make equations that way, though."

Yuri   "Let alone systems of equations, I guess."

Me   "Right. So once we've decided there are x cranes and y turtles, we sit back and think, 'What's the relationship between x and y?' That's the first step in setting up an equation. That's what an equation is, after all, a statement of the relationship between unknowns, and this is the key to using math to solve this kind of problem. Your trick of starting out with all cranes, then adding turtles into the mix is a cool one. But learning how to represent unknowns as letters, and how to show the relationship between unknowns as equations, that's important too."

            Yuri blinks.

Me   "Still with me?"

Yuri   "I'm good."

Me   "You're smart enough to read this problem and just come up with an answer, but not all problems will be so easy. That's why you need to learn how to do them using these steps."

Yuri   "I'll buy that."

Me   "Start by assigning variables to the unknowns. Decide what x and y will stand for, then think about how they're related. That will let you describe their relationship as an equation."

Yuri   "And?"

Me   "Well, once you have an equation everything should fall into place. Just use the algebra rules you've learned to solve for the variables. Finally, remember what x and y stood for in the first place, and you have your answer. More generally, it works like this."

Solving Problems With Math

1. Take the problem from "the real world" to "the math world."

2. Solve the problem in the math world.

3. Bring the answer from the math world back to the real world.

Yuri   "Never thought of it that way, but yeah, makes sense."

Me   "For this problem, step 1 was setting up the equations. Then step 2 was solving them. Not so hard in leg counting problems; the system of equations is pretty simple. But like I said, learning this pattern of moving back and forth between the real world and the math world is the true goal."

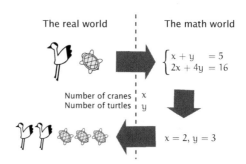

Moving between worlds

Yuri   "The math world! I like it! I wonder why they don't teach
            it to us like this in school?"

Me   "They probably are, you just—"

Mom   "Snack time!"

My mother shouted from the kitchen, cutting short our math talk. I
could have gone on, but nothing came between Yuri and her snacks.

" ... and problem solvers bring answers from other realms."

PROBLEMS FOR CHAPTER 2

Problem 2-1 (Mathematical descriptions)

Use mathematical notation to represent the number of legs between x cranes and y turtles.

(Answer on page 134)

Problem 2-2 (Mathematical descriptions)

Use mathematical notation to represent the number of legs between x animals that have a legs each, and y animals that have b legs each.

(Answer on page 134)

Problem 2-3 (Solving systems of equations)

Solve the following system of equations:

$$\begin{cases} x + y = 6 \\ 2x + 3y = 14 \end{cases}$$

(Answer on page 135)

Problem 2-4 (Solving systems of equations)

Solve the following system of equations:

$$\begin{cases} x + y & = 99999 \\ 2x + 4y & = 375306 \end{cases}$$

(Answer on page 135)

CHAPTER 3

Equations and Silhouettes

"Problem solvers know what to look
at..."

3.1 CLEAR EYES

Sometimes I couldn't help but wonder if I was really seeing things clearly.

Only a fool judges things by their appearance. Wisdom lies in learning to see their true nature. Miruka once called it "learning to see the structure of things."

I wanted to see those structures. I wanted eyes clear enough to see what was important, and what wasn't.

Heading to the library after class, I found Tetra writing furiously.

3.2 SECRET NOTEBOOK

Me   "Hey, Tetra. What's up?"

Tetra   "Hey! Just doing a bit of work."

Me   "And working hard, it looks like. What is that, homework?"

Tetra   "No, just updating my notebook."

Me   "Your math notebook?"

Tetra   "Well, *a* math notebook. This one isn't for school,
           though. It's for me. This is my secret notebook, where
           I write down all the math you and Miruka teach me so
           I don't forget. I'm such a scatterbrain, if I don't write
           everything down I know I'll forget it."

Me   "I don't think you're a scatterbrain."

Tetra   "Nice try, but let's be real. Anyway, I figure if I keep
           everything in one place, I can just whip it out whenever
           I need it!"

           Tetra whips out the notebook to demonstrate.

Me   "Not a bad idea. Just organizing and writing every-
           thing out makes for some good studying, too. One thing,
           though."

Tetra   "What's that?"

Me   "It isn't much of a secret notebook if you tell everyone
           about it."

Tetra   "Uh, right. Forget I said anything!"

           Tetra blushes.

Me   "Consider it forgotten."

3.3 How to Write Equations

Tetra   "Remember how the other day we were talking about
           how math changes?"

Me   "Mmm, vaguely."

Tetra   "About how the numbers start to fade away, and math
           becomes more about letters."

Me   "Ah, right. Yeah, when all those x's and y's start creeping in, that's when the real math starts."

Tetra   "All those letters made me really nervous back in junior high. Something about them makes the math look harder. Well, not something simple like $x + 5$, I guess. That's just adding 5 to something you don't know the number for yet. I can deal with that. But then things get so much more complicated."

Me   "It's not so bad, once you get used to it."

Tetra   "I still remember $3x^2$ knocking me for a loop."

Me   "What about it?"

Tetra   "Well, $3x$ is 3 times x, right?

Me   "Sure."

Tetra   "And we learned that the small 2 tells you how many times to multiply something. So I couldn't understand why $3x^2$ didn't mean to multiply two $3x$'s."

Me   "Ah, I see."

Tetra   "Of course now I know that $3x^2$ doesn't mean to multiply two $3x$'s together, it means to multiply 3 and x^2 with each other. In other words, 3 times x times x."

$$3x^2 = 3 \times \underbrace{x \times x}_{\text{two } x\text{'s}}$$

Me   "That's right. You can also say $3x^2$ means $3(x^2)$, not $(3x)^2$. It's three x^2's."

$$3x^2 = 3(x^2) = \underbrace{x^2 + x^2 + x^2}_{\text{three } x^2\text{'s}}$$

Tetra   "I guess I missed it when the teacher explained it that way."

Me	"It's easy to get distracted when something doesn't quite click."
Tetra	"Which is pretty much all the time for me. But I'll never forget this $3x^2$ thing. I got so many problems wrong because of that."
Me	"But you've got it down now. See? You aren't scatter-brained."
Tetra	"I don't know. You wouldn't believe how long it took me to catch on to what I was doing wrong."
Me	"It's not about speed, it's about persistence, and nobody's got you beat there. There are lots of people who give up on math just because they get confused by the basics. The rules for writing equations aren't complicated, but it still takes practice before you get used to them. And if you stop practicing, you'll forget it all pretty quick. That tricks a lot of people into thinking they aren't good at math, or that they aren't a 'math person,' whatever that means."
Tetra	"Well now you've got me worried. I'm pretty sure I haven't had enough practice writing equations. Can you help me brush up?"

3.4 WRITING POLYNOMIALS

Me	"Well, when I say equations, I really mean polynomials. For example, can you write out $3x^2 - 2x - 8$, using multiplication symbols?"

$$3x^2 - 2x - 8$$

Tetra	"I think so, sure."

$$3x^2 \qquad - 2x \quad - 8$$
$$= 3 \times x \times x - 2 \times x - 8$$

Me   "Perfect."

Tetra   "That's a relief.

Me   "Lots of people prefer to use a dot instead of this multi-plication symbol, though, probably because it looks too much like an x, which can be confusing."

Tetra   "Like this, you mean?"

$$3x^2 \quad - 2x \quad - 8$$
$$= 3 \cdot x \cdot x - 2 \cdot x - 8$$

Me   "Exactly like that. Now let's try going the other way. Can you write this without the multiplication dots?"

$$x \cdot x \cdot x + 4 \cdot x \cdot x - x + 2 \cdot x \cdot x \cdot x + 6$$

Tetra   "Hmm. Just count the number of x's being multiplied."

$$\underbrace{x \cdot x \cdot x}_{\text{three x's}} + 4 \cdot \underbrace{x \cdot x}_{\text{two x's}} - x + 2 \cdot \underbrace{x \cdot x \cdot x}_{\text{three x's}} + 6$$

Me   "Right."

Tetra   "There's three, then two, then three . . . so you write it like this!"

$$\underbrace{x \cdot x \cdot x}_{\text{three x's}} + 4 \cdot \underbrace{x \cdot x}_{\text{two x's}} - x + 2 \cdot \underbrace{x \cdot x \cdot x}_{\text{three x's}} + 6$$
$$= x^3 \qquad + 4x^2 \qquad - x + 2x^3 \qquad + 6$$

Me   "Right, using exponents is a great way to tighten things up. There's still a bit more cleaning up to do, though."

Tetra   "Oh yeah?"

Me   "See how there are two cubes? The terms with x^3 in
            them? It's best to combine the x^3 and the $2x^3$ here
            into $3x^3$."

$$x \cdot x \cdot x + 4 \cdot x \cdot x - x + 2 \cdot x \cdot x \cdot x + 6$$
$$= \underline{x^3} + 4x^2 - x + \underline{2x^3} + 6$$
$$= \underline{3x^3} + 4x^2 - x + 6 \qquad \text{combine } x^3 \text{ and } 2x^3 \text{ into } 3x^3$$

Tetra   "Ah, right. I knew that."

Me   "This is called combining like terms. 'Like terms' means
            terms that have the same variable raised to the same
            power."

Like terms

- x^3 and $2x^3$ are like terms (they're both terms with a cubed
  variable x).

- $3x^3$ and $4x^2$ are *not* like terms (same variable, but raised
  to different powers).

- y^3 and $2x^3$ are *not* like terms (same exponent, but different variables).

Tetra   "This is exactly the kind of thing that I keep in my secret
            notebook, so I can look over it again later."

Me   "Then you should add something about descending pow-
            ers, too. See how we ordered the four terms in $3x^3 +
            4x^2 - x + 6$, with the highest exponents on x coming
            first? That's called writing with descending powers, and
            it's how you should usually write polynomials."

$$\underbrace{3x^3}_{\text{3rd degree term}} + \underbrace{4x^2}_{\text{2nd degree term}} + \underbrace{-x}_{\text{1st degree term}} + \underbrace{6}_{\text{0th degree term}}$$

Tetra   "Hang on, writing all this down..."

Writing polynomials

- Use exponents
  (Example: write $x \cdot x \cdot x$ as x^3)

- Combine like terms
  (Example: write $x^3 + 2x^3$ as $3x^3$)

- Write terms with descending powers
  (Example: Order terms like $x^3 \to x^2 \to x \to$ constants)

Me   "That's a good summary."

Tetra raises her hand.

Tetra   "One question."

Me   "Sure, anything."

Tetra   "I think I understand these rules. But what I don't get is . . . why? Why do we need to write polynomials like this in the first place?"

A sudden appearance saves me from Tetra's insightful question.

Tetra   "Hi, Miruka!"

3.5 WHY WE WRITE POLYNOMIALS THIS WAY

Miruka   "What's today's topic?"

Tetra   "Equations! Well, polynomials, I guess. And how to write them."

Miruka   "Hmm."

Miruka pushes up her glasses.

Tetra   "We're talking about combining like terms, and descending powers, and we were just about to talk about why we should always—"

Miruka   "Confirmation of identity."

Tetra   "Confirm—huh?"

Miruka   "If nothing else, it helps you to compare two polynomials for sameness."

Tetra   "And that's confirming their identity?"

             Tetra tilts her head. She never pretends to understand something she doesn't. It's one of the things I like about her.

Miruka   "Right. One of the reasons we write polynomials the way we do is to make it easier to compare two polynomials and see if they're the same. That's not all, though."

             Miruka raises a finger.

Miruka   "Pop quiz."

Problem

Are the following two polynomials equivalent?

$$x^2 + 3x^2 + x + 1 \qquad 2 + 2x + 4x^2 - x - 1$$

Tetra   "Well, they look different, but . . ."

Me   "Just clean them both up, see what happens."

Tetra   "Oh, right. Okay, I'll start with the one on the left."

$$x^2 + 3x^2 + x + 1$$
$$= 4x^2 + x + 1 \qquad \text{combine like terms } x^2 \text{ and } 3x^2$$

Tetra   "Okay, now for the other one."

$$2 + 2x + 4x^2 - x - 1$$
$$= 2 + x + 4x^2 - 1 \qquad \text{combine like terms } 2x \text{ and } -x$$
$$= 1 + x + 4x^2 \qquad \text{combine constants } 2 \text{ and } -1$$
$$= 4x^2 + x + 1 \qquad \text{order by descending powers}$$

Me   "There you go."

Tetra   "Oh, cool! They both became $4x^2 + x + 1$! So that means they're equal to each other, right?"

Miruka   "It does. To use the proper wording, though, the two polynomials are 'identically equal.'"

Answer

The following two polynomials are equal identically:

$$x^2 + 3x^2 + x + 1 \qquad\qquad 2 + 2x + 4x^2 - x - 1$$
$$= 4x^2 + x + 1 \qquad\qquad\quad = 4x^2 + x + 1$$

Tetra writes in her notebook as she speaks.

Tetra   "'Equal identically'? That's different from just plain 'equals'?"

Miruka   "It means that the polynomials will be equal for any value of the variable x."

Tetra   "Oh, okay—no, not okay. What exactly does that mean?"

Miruka   "Take the two terms $2x$ and $3x$. If you let x be 0, then both of these terms will be 0 too, right?"

Tetra   "Right."

Miruka   "But what happens if you let x be 1? Then $2x = 2$ and $3x = 3$, so they aren't equal."

Tetra   "Ah, I see!"

Miruka   "So $2x$ and $3x$ aren't identically equal."

Tetra   "Okay, so two things are identically equal when they're equal for *any* value, not just particular ones."

Miruka   "Precisely."

Miruka pauses briefly before speaking again.

Miruka   "The rules for writing polynomials ensure that they stick to a standard form. Part of that is to make them easier to compare, like we've been talking about, but descending powers also makes it easier to check their degree."

Tetra   "Their degree. Like whether they're linear or quadratic and all that?"

Miruka   "Right. When a polynomial is written with descending powers, you can just look at the exponent on the first term to read off the polynomial's degree."

$\underline{2x} + 1$ $2x$ has exponent 1; linear (1st degree) polynomial

$\underline{3x^2} + 2x + 1$ $3x^2$ has exponent 2; quadratic (2nd degree) polynomial

$\underline{x^3} + 3x^2 + 2x + 1$ x^3 has exponent 3; cubic (3rd degree) polynomial

Me   "And the degree of a polynomial is kind of a big deal."

Miruka   "Which makes for another pop quiz."

Problem

What's the big deal about the degree of a polynomial?

Tetra   "I have absolutely no idea."

Miruka   "No?"

Tetra "I know about linear equations and quadratics and cubics and all that—we studied those in class. But you're asking why it's important that we distinguish between them, right? I've never even thought about that."

Miruka points at me.

Miruka "What do *you* think?"

Me "I think the degree of a polynomial is important because it tells you a lot about how the polynomial behaves. Close enough?"

Miruka "I guess. At a minimum you can say that two polynomials of the same degree will have similar characteristics. There are other answers to the problem, though, depending on how you're looking at things."

(One Possible) Answer

The degree of a polynomial is important because polynomials with the same degree will also have the same characteristics.

Me "I'll buy that."

Miruka "Which of course raises the question—"

Tetra "—just what *are* these 'characteristics' that the degree of a polynomial tells you about?"

3.6 GRAPHING LINEAR FUNCTIONS

Miruka "It'll be easier to see the characteristics of these polynomials if we use them to create and graph some functions. A linear polynomial's graph, for example, will always be a straight line."

Me "Examples *are* the key to understanding."

Miruka   "Exactly. Now quick, graph a linear function."

Miruka points at me again.

Me   "Okay, x on the horizontal axis, y on the vertical. Just your typical coordinate plane."

The coordinate plane

Me   "I like to label the intersection with an 'O'."

Tetra   "Why an 'O'?"

Miruka   "For 'origin.'"

Tetra   "Oh, of course."

Miruka   "Carry on."

Me   "Right. So anyway, I guess the simplest linear equation—or first degree equation, if you want to think of it that way—would be just looking at x itself. So let's graph the linear equation $y = x$."

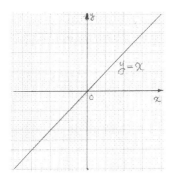

A graph of the 1st degree equation $y = x$

Tetra   "I remember this, but maybe we used simpler words. This is what Miruka meant when she said linear polynomials will have straight line graphs, right?"

Me   "Yep."

Miruka   "More examples."

Me   "Yes, ma'am."

I draw a few more graphs of linear equations.

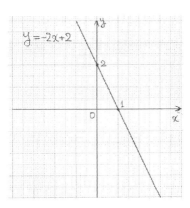

A graph of the 1st degree equation $y = -2x + 2$

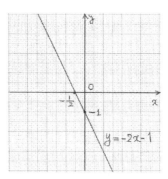

A graph of the 1st degree equation $y = -2x - 1$

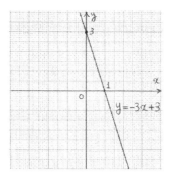

A graph of the 1st degree equation $y = -3x + 3$

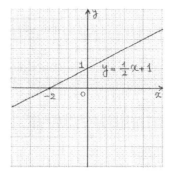

A graph of the 1st degree equation $y = \dfrac{1}{2}x + 1$

Tetra   "Yep, they're all straight lines."

Miruka   "Each of these is a different equation, but their degree is the same."

$$y = x \qquad \text{1st degree equation}$$
$$y = -2x + 2 \qquad \text{1st degree equation}$$
$$y = -2x - 1 \qquad \text{1st degree equation}$$
$$y = -3x + 3 \qquad \text{1st degree equation}$$
$$y = \frac{1}{2}x + 1 \qquad \text{1st degree equation}$$

Tetra   "And having the same degree is what makes them all lines."

Miruka   "Right. That's one of the reasons an equation's degree is important; same degree, same basic shape."

Tetra looks at the graph.

Tetra   "Well, I *guess* you can call a straight line a shape . . ."

3.7 Graphing Second Degree Equations

Miruka   "Tetra has a point. Doing this with just straight lines is pretty boring."

Me   "A second degree equation, then?"

Tetra   "Yes, please!"

Me   "Okay, we'll start with the simplest second degree equation, using just x^2. We'll turn that into $y = x^2$ for graphing. It should be a parabola going through $(0, 0)$, $(1, 1)$, and $(2, 4)$, but graphing this is harder than it looks."

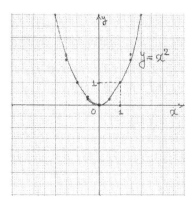

A graph of the 2nd degree equation $y = x^2$

Miruka   "What a mess."

Me   "Hey, this ain't easy. Here, second draft."

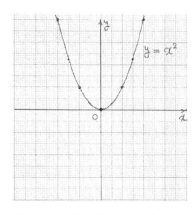

A second attempt at a graph of the 2nd degree equation $y = x^2$

Miruka   "Better. Now try lowering it."

Me   "No problem. I'll just graph the second degree function $y = x^2 - 1$ instead."

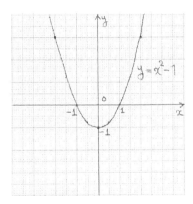

A graph of the 2nd degree equation $y = x^2 - 1$

Miruka "Okay. Now can you move it to the right?"

Me "To the right, huh? Let's see. Oh, I know. Just add a first degree term, like $y = x^2 - 2x$."

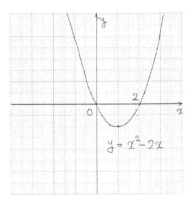

A graph of the 2nd degree equation $y = x^2 - 2x$

Tetra "Whoa, that was out of the blue."

Me "Nah, just think about the intersections with the x-axis. See how the parabola $y = x^2 - 1$ crosses the x-axis in two places, where x is 1, and where it's −1? If you want to move the entire parabola to the right by one, those points have to become $\underline{0}$ and $\underline{2}$. So we just need the second degree equation made from $(x - \underline{0})(x - \underline{2})$. From that, $(x - 0)(x - 2) = x(x - 2) = x^2 - 2x$, so I used $y = x^2 - 2x$."

Miruka   "Another way to put it would be to say you replaced the x in $y = x^2 - 1$ with $x - 1$, and used that to create $y = (x - 1)^2 - 1$."

Tetra   "I'll, uh . . . think about this some more later."

Miruka   "Gimme a narrower parabola next, one that's concave down."

Me   "To flip it over, we just have to make the coefficient on the second degree term negative. And for the parabola to get narrower, I guess the values we're plotting have to change more quickly, which means a different coefficient. I'll try using -2."

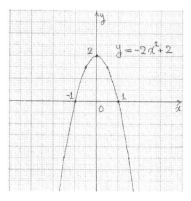

A graph of the 2nd degree equation $y = -2x^2 + 2$

Tetra   "Concave down, huh. This is all vaguely familiar."

Miruka   "Still kind of messy, but I *guess* we can call that a parabola."

Tetra lets out a loud cry of excitement.

Me   "What is it?"

Tetra   "I get it! I totally get parabolas now!"

Me   "Get what about them?"

Tetra   "We learned about second degree equations in class. I
            even graphed parabolas like this. But somehow I never
            thought of them as being the same thing."

Me   "And that's what got you so excited?"

Tetra   "Kinda. But it's more like, I dunno, I caught a glimpse
            into the world of math or something."

            Tetra shrugs.

Tetra   "Like, there's this math world out there that *really ex-
            ists*. Linear equations and quadratic equations, and a
            million equations I've never even heard of. It felt like
            that graph opened a door and gave me a glimpse of this
            whole new world, one I'd never seen before. I'm sorry, I
            know that doesn't make any sense."

Miruka   "It makes perfect sense. You attained a higher viewpoint
            through the use of specific examples. Here's a summary
            of what we've discussed."

Graphs of first and second degree functions

- The graph of a function created from a first degree equation is a straight line.

- The graph of a function created from a second degree
  equation is a parabola.

Miruka   "But it doesn't end there. The graph of a function cre-
              ated from a third degree equation has its own particular
              shape, and so does one from a fourth degree equation,
              and so on."

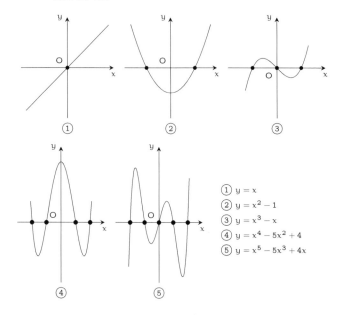

① $y = x$
② $y = x^2 - 1$
③ $y = x^3 - x$
④ $y = x^4 - 5x^2 + 4$
⑤ $y = x^5 - 5x^3 + 4x$

              Tetra nods.

Miruka   "There's a close connection between a polynomial's de-
              gree and the graph of its function, but that's just one ex-
              ample of why degrees are important. Even Euler spent a
              lot of time studying the relation between equations and
              their curves. Of course, Euler was all over the place, so
              I guess that's no surprise."

Miruka was a huge fan of Leonhard Euler, one of the most productive
mathematicians in history. She got a sparkle in her eye whenever she
talked about him.

Tetra   "We strayed pretty far from how to write equations, but
              this is neat stuff. First degree equations, second degree
              equations, third degree equations, x, x^2, x^3. There's so
              much to study!"

Miruka   "Just be sure to remember that the degree of a polyno-
            mial is important information if you want to know what
            its graph looks like. Details like the coefficients on them
            are usually just fluff. Get rid of all that, and the degree
            still tells you the the equation's general shape. You can
            even tell how many solutions it will have."

Tetra   "It's like a silhouette!"

Miruka   "A silhouette?"

Tetra   "When you said you can get rid of all the details, it re-
            minded me of silhouettes. They don't have all the details
            of a normal picture, but you can still see the basic shape
            that made them!"

Miruka   "The silhouette of an equation. I like it."

Ms. Mizutani "The library is *closed*!"

      Our math talk for the day ends.

" ... and problem solvers know what not to look at."

PROBLEMS FOR CHAPTER 3

Problem 3-1 (Writing polynomials)

Simplify the following, referring to the discussion on page 43:

$$1 + 2x + 3x^3 - 4x + 5x^2 + 6$$

(Answer on page 137)

Problem 3-2 (Writing polynomials)

Simplify the following, referring to the discussion on page 43:

$$1x^3 + 3x^1 - 5x^2 - 4x + 2x^2 + 2x^2$$

Be sure to pay attention to the following:

- Coefficients of 1 normally aren't written. (Example: $1x^3$ is normally written as x^3.)

- Exponents of 1 normally aren't written. (Example: $3x^1$ is normally written as $3x$.)

(Answer on page 137)

Problem 3-3 (Degree of polynomials)

What is the degree of the following polynomial on x?

$$x^3 + x^2 - x^3 + x - 1$$

(Answer on page 138)

Problem 3-4 (Graphs of first degree equations)

Draw a graph of the following first degree equation:

$$y = 2x - 4$$

(Answer on page 139)

Problem 3-5 (Graphs of second degree equations)

Draw a graph of the following second degree equation:

$$y = -x^2 + 1$$

(Answer on page 140)

CHAPTER 4

Proportions and Inverse Proportions

"Problem solvers never overlook
changes..."

4.1 SINCERITY

Tetra was the most sincere girl I knew. She listened sincerely, she
thought sincerely, she spoke sincerely. It was her most powerful
weapon when studying. But that isn't to say she was simple. She
often had flashes of insight that were truly unique, and that was
something wonderful.

As I was pondering such things, Yuri decided to drop in for a
visit.

4.2 IN MY ROOM

Yuri   "Yo, what's up?"

Me   "What's up with you? You look exhausted."

Yuri   "Late night gaming. I hit a super hard boss, and I
          couldn't let it go."

Me   "Glad to see you've got your priorities straight."

Yuri   "Hey, lay off. It just so happens I'm here for some tutor-
            ing. Tell me everything there is to know about graphs."

Me   "In a hundred words or less?"

Yuri   "Whatever it takes. My teacher's been all hyped about
            how important graphs are lately, but he leaves out the
            details, like *why* they're important."

Me   "Hmm. What kind of graphs are we talking about here?"

Yuri   "There's more than one?"

Me   "Plenty more."

Yuri   "Well then, ones like this, I guess."

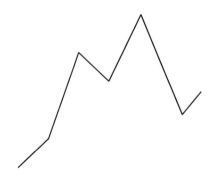

Me   "That's, what? A dancing 'M'?"

            Yuri punches me in the shoulder.

Yuri   "It's a line graph!"

Me   "I'd say it's *part* of a line graph. Here's the rest."

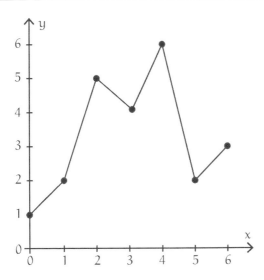

Yuri   "Details, details."

Me   "But important ones."

Two basic graphing rules

- Draw axes with names like x and y.

- Include units on your axes.

Me   "In this graph I've named the horizontal axis x and the vertical axis y, but that won't always be the case. Any time you read or write a graph, be sure you know exactly what each of the axes represents."

Yuri   "I know, my teacher is always saying that."

Me   "Well, your teacher is right about one thing: graphs are important."

Yuri   "The question is, *why* are they important?"

Me	"Well, for one thing they let you visualize change."
Yuri	"I don't even understand what that means."
Me	"It's not that hard an idea. It just means looking at how the amount of something is changing as time goes by."
Yuri	"Like how what changes?"
Me	"I dunno, like your weight for example."
Yuri	"You have *got* to get some new math examples to use with girls."

4.3 LINE GRAPHS

Me	"Fine, we'll use temperature instead. You'll see line graphs that show changes in temperature all the time."

I do a quick web search and print out a couple of pages.

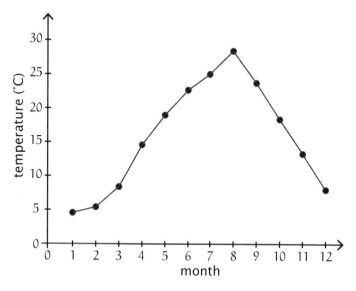

Average temperatures in Tokyo

Me   "Check this out. This is a graph of temperatures in Tokyo
            a few years back."

Yuri   "And historical weather reports are interesting how?"

Me   "The trends. See how the temperature goes up from Jan-
            uary to August, then back down from August to Decem-
            ber?"

Yuri   "You mean it's hot in summer, and cold in winter? Wow!
            Without math, how would we ever know these things?"

Me   "It's not just that. Check out the shape of the graph.
            See how it peaks in August? That means August is the
            hottest month. That's not so obvious from just going
            outside, but you can read it off this graph at a glance."

Yuri   "Reading? From a graph?"

Me   "Sure. Sort of like how you can read between the lines
            when you're reading text."

Yuri   "Hmm, maybe."

Me   "Another important thing about graphs is units. The
            units for temperature in this graph is degrees Celsius."

Yuri   "I remain unconvinced."

Me   "About what?"

Yuri   "About how graphs are telling me things I don't already
            know."

Me   "Well check this one out."

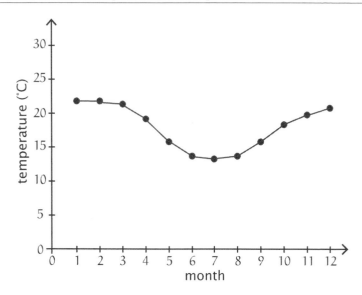

Yuri   "You must have done the math wrong. This one says that
            summer is cold and winter is hot."

Me   "Nope. This graph shows the temperature of Sydney,
            Australia. That's in the southern hemisphere, so the
            temperature trends are the opposite of Tokyo's. See how
            the graph tells you that July is the coldest month there?"

Yuri   "Another example of reading between the line graphs, I
            suppose."

Me   "One of many possible examples."

        Yuri coils a lock of hair around her finger.

Yuri   "It doesn't tell me the exact temperature, though. It
            looks like it's around 12°C, but I can't be sure."

Me   "Good point. This isn't an ideal graph for reading precise
            values. If that's what you're after, then a table might be
            better."

Temperatures in Tokyo and Sydney (°C)

	1	2	3	4	5	6	7	8	9	10	11	12
Tokyo	5.1	5.7	8.4	14.2	18.5	21.8	25.1	27.2	23.1	17.7	12.5	8.0
Sydney	22.5	22.8	21.3	18.9	15.6	13.2	12.1	13.3	15.4	18.1	19.6	21.8

Yuri   "Okay, let's see. The average temperature in Tokyo in
          July is 25.1°C, and in Sydney it's 12.1°C."

Me   "An example of reading things from a table."

Yuri   "Smart, ain't I."

Me   "The takeaway here is that graphs are good for seeing
          the overall shape of things, and tables are best for giving
          specific values. Which to use depends on what your goal
          is."

Yuri   "Which should I use if my goal is world domination?"

4.4 INVERSE PROPORTIONS

Me   "Let's   forget   about   temperatures—and   world
          domination—and   play   with   a   more   mathematical
          graph."

Yuri   "What, these aren't 'mathematical' enough?"

Me   "Have you ever heard of proportions?"

Yuri   "Sure. Like one thing growing in proportion to another?"

Me   "Right. So do you know the definition of a proportion?"

Yuri   "The definition, like from a dictionary?"

Me   "I'm looking for the mathematical definition, which is a
          little more precise. You know how important precision is
          in math, right? You have to be really careful about the
          words you use, to be sure that everyone knows exactly
          what you mean. You can't use words in a vague sense, or
          the whole thing falls apart. That makes definitions one
          of the most important things in mathematics."

Yuri   "Mom says passing my classes is the most important thing."

Me   "That'll be much easier to do when you understand definitions."

Yuri   "Well then, count me in. I'm gonna define the heck out of everything from now on."

Me   "Okay, start by trying to define the heck out of 'proportion.'"

Yuri   "A proportion is ... um ... when one thing gets crazy big, something else gets crazy big too. Done."

Me   "Uh ..."

Yuri   "You have that 'not quite' look."

Me   "Yeah. Something getting 'crazy big' doesn't cut it."

Yuri   "Sounds pretty clear to me."

Me   "How about this to start with: you have a quantity x and a quantity y, and when x doubles or triples or quadruples, then y doubles or triples or quadruples too. In that case, you can say that y is proportional to x."

Yuri   "That's what I just said!"

Me   "No, you just said something about getting crazy big. You didn't say anything specific about how big things are getting."

Yuri   "But that's what I meant."

Me   "Not good enough. Not for math, anyway. You've gotta say exactly what you mean."

Yuri   "Stupid rules . . ."

Me   "Let's get rid of the vagueness, and give a *precise* definition of proportions."

Definition of proportion

Assume a quantity x, a quantity y, and a nonzero constant a for which the following relationship holds:

$$y = ax.$$

Then y is proportional to x.

Yuri   "That says the same thing as all that doubling and tripling stuff?"

Me   "It does."

Yuri   "You sure?"

Me   "Well, assuming that $y = ax$, what happens to y when $x = 10$?"

Yuri   "No clue."

Me   "Maybe try a little? The relationship between x and y is that $y = ax$, right? So if $x = 10$, what's y?"

Yuri   "Like I said, I don't know. Because I don't know what a is!"

Me   "Oh, okay. I see what's confusing you now, but don't worry about it. Just let a be a. Since you know that $y = ax$ will always be true, if $x = 10$ then y must be $10a$."

$$
\begin{aligned}
y &= ax && \text{definition of proportion} \\
&= a \times x && ax \text{ means } a \times x \\
&= a \times 10 && \text{let } x = 10 \text{ as an example} \\
&= 10a && \times \text{ sign omitted; write 10 first}
\end{aligned}
$$

Yuri   "Okay, I get it now."

Me   "Then what is y when $x = 20$?"

Yuri   "Erm ... y = 20a, I guess?"

Me   "You're right, though you lack your usual confidence."

Yuri   "It'll be back. Just give it some time. What's next?"

Me   "Well, you see that if x = 10, then y = 10a, and if x = 20 then y = 20a, right? So if x doubles, then y will double too. Because 10a doubled is 20a."

Yuri   "Yeah, I guess that would be double, wouldn't it."

Me   "It would. If you say that y = ax, then you can start with x = 10, and increase x to 20 or 30 or 40 or whatever, and y will increase with it, to 20a or 30a or 40a, and so on. There's your doubling and tripling and all that."

Yuri   "Hmm..."

Me   "Maybe another graph will help."

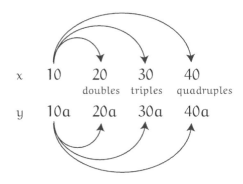

Yuri   "Still hmm..."

Me   "A table would be better, maybe?"

Table showing the relation y = ax

x	10	20	30	40
y	10a	20a	30a	40a

Yuri   "Hrm..."

Me   "What is it that's still not clicking?"

Yuri   "It's just...you said that when $y = ax$, y is proportional to x, right?"

Me   "Right."

Yuri   "Then you wrote this table where x is 10 and 20 and 30 and all, but what about when x is 1, or 2? Everything should work then, too, shouldn't it?"

Me   "Yep. And it'll work when x is 3.4, or when x is 56.789, or when x is anything."

Yuri   "Why those numbers?"

Me   "First ones to pop into my head."

Yuri   "Okay, I'm good then. So when $y = ax$, y is proportional to x, and that's how proportions are defined."

Me   "Perfect. But there's just a bit more."

            Yuri sighs.

Yuri   "There always is, isn't there."

4.5 GRAPHING PROPORTIONS AND LINES THROUGH THE ORIGIN

Me   "If you say y is proportional to x, then you're saying the relationship $y = ax$ holds. If you graph that, you'll always get a straight line through the origin. You know what the origin of a graph is?"

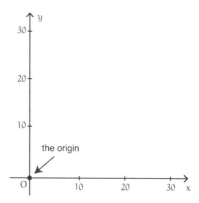

Yuri	"We learned that, like, forever ago."
Me	"Okay, then let's start by letting $a = 1$ and plotting the graph of $y = ax$. Since a is 1, we're just plotting $y = x$, which is really simple; when $x = 1$, $y = 1$, and when $x = 2$, $y = 2$, and so on, because x and y are always the same value, right?"

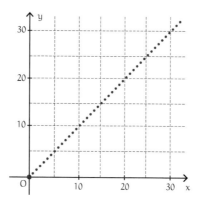

What happens to $y = ax$ when $a = 1$?

Yuri	"All those dots are going to make a straight line, right?"
Me	"Not just that. They'll form a straight line that goes through the origin."

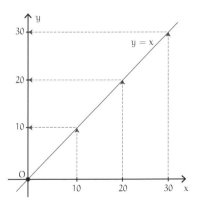

Graph of $y = ax$ when $a = 1$

Yuri   "What's with the arrows?"

Me   "I'm trying to show the y values you get from the x values. So like when x is 10, you go straight up until you hit the graph, then turn left and go until you hit the 10 on the y-axis."

Yuri   "Good idea."

Me   "Glad you approve. Let's do this again when $a = 2$. Since $y = ax$, that means we'll be graphing $y = 2x$, right?"

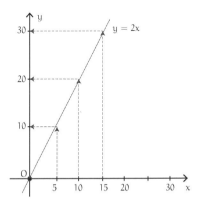

Graph of $y = ax$ when $a = 2$

Me   "Right through the origin again."

Yuri   "Maybe it just got lucky."

Me   "Think so? Then let's try again, with $a = 0.5$."

Yuri smirks.

Yuri   "I was hoping you'd say that."

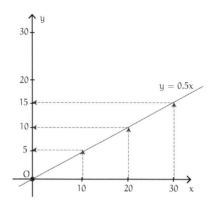

Graph of $y = ax$ when $a = 0.5$

Me   "Three in a row now. Satisfied? Any graph of a proportion will go through the origin. You can say the reverse, too. Any graph that's a straight line going through the origin will be the graph of a proportion."

Yuri   "Interesting."

Me   "This is another example of *reading* graphs instead of just looking at them. When we see a straight line passing through the origin, we can read between the lines and learn something about the relationship between x and y. Like that y is proportional to x."

Checking a graph to see if it's a proportion

- Is the graph a straight line?

- Does the graph pass through the origin?

If the answer to both of the above is yes, then y is proportional to x. If the answer to either of the above is no, then y is not proportional to x.

Me   "There are certain graph shapes you'll want to keep an eye out for. Just like there are important equation shapes."

Yuri   "Equations have shapes?"

Me   "Sure. Take $y = ax$, for example."

$$y = ax$$

Me   "If x in this equation is 0, then you know y is 0 too, right?"

Yuri   "Gotta be, since 0 times anything is 0."

Me   "Specifics."

            Yuri rolls her eyes.

Yuri   "If you say that x is 0 then the equation says y is $a \times 0$. So y has to be 0, because 0 times anything is 0."

Me   "Good. So you know that if x is 0, y is 0 too. But think about it. Doesn't that mean $(0, 0)$ has to be on the graph of the equation $y = ax$?"

Yuri   "Well whaddaya know. Now you're reading things about the graph off of the equation."

Me   "Check out this graph. Tell me, is y proportional to x?"

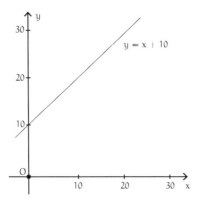

Is y proportional to x?

Yuri   "Well, I guess when x gets huge y would get huge too,
            but ..."

Me   "But what?"

Yuri   "Hang on! We had a checklist for this, didn't we."

Checking a graph to see if it's a proportion

- Is the graph a straight line?   **YES!**

- Does the graph pass through the origin?   **NO!**

Yuri   "So it isn't proportional!"

Me   "Well done. This graph doesn't pass through the origin,
            and that's enough to tell you it isn't the graph of a pro-
            portion."

Yuri   "Okay, I think I've got this down. Since y is proportional
            to x, when x doubles y doubles too, and when x triples
            y triples too. So x and y get bigger in the same way—uh
            oh, there's that look again."

Me   "Not quite."

Yuri	"I knew it."
Me	"Don't forget that a can be negative. That would mean that when x gets bigger, y would get smaller."
Yuri	"Smaller? Even though they're proportional?"
Me	"Yep. Here, check out this graph."

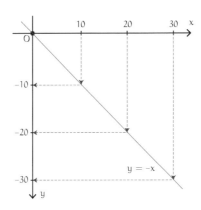

Graphs going down can be proportions too

Yuri	"It's going down."
Me	"But it's still a proportion, mathematically speaking, even when y gets smaller as x gets bigger."
Yuri	"Yeah, I guess it still passes the checklist."
Me	"Just be sure to note that the scale of things hasn't changed. Doubling or tripling x is still doubling or tripling y."
Yuri	"So is a line going down like this what they call an inverse proportion?"
Me	"No, that's different."
Yuri	"Different how?"

Me   "The graph of an inverse proportion is a hyperbola, like
            this."

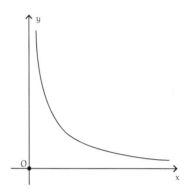

Graph of an inverse proportion

4.6 PROPORTIONS AND INVERSE PROPORTIONS

Yuri   "That doesn't make sense."

Me   "Why not?"

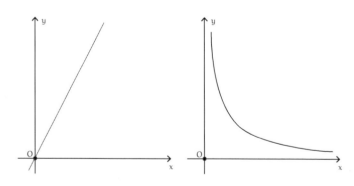

Graphs of a proportion (left) and an inverse proportion (right)

Yuri   "I dunno, it just doesn't seem *balanced* somehow. It
            would make more sense if proportions went up and in-
            verse proportions went down."

Me   "Let's check out why inverse proportions look like this and see if it doesn't make more sense then."

Yuri   "So what's the definition this time?"

Me   "Before we define inverse proportions, let's review the definition of a proportion."

Definition of proportion

Assume a quantity x, a quantity y, and a nonzero constant a for which the following relationship holds:

$$y = ax.$$

Then y is proportional to x.

Yuri   "And the definition of an inverse proportion?"

Me   "Ask and ye shall receive."

Definition of inverse proportion

Assume a quantity x, a quantity y, and a nonzero constant a for which the following relationship holds:

$$y = \frac{a}{x}.$$

Then y is inversely proportional to x.

Yuri   "Seriously?"

Me   "What's wrong? Do you understand the definition?"

Yuri   "Sure I do. You have a constant a, and y is a divided by x."

Me   "Right, and that means y is inversely proportional to x. You can also say 'x and y are in inverse proportion.'"

Yuri   "Still not clicking, though."

Me   "No? A proportion is $y = ax$, an inverse proportion is $y = \dfrac{a}{x}$. It makes all the difference in the graphs, when you're dividing by x instead of multiplying."

Comparison of proportions and inverse proportions

$y = ax$ Equation for a y that's proportional to x

$y = \dfrac{a}{x}$ Equation for a y that's inversely proportional to x

---

Yuri   "Yeah, I know that's what the equations say, but still ..."

Me   "What's bugging you?"

Yuri   "I'm not sure how to put it into words."

Me   "Well, while you're looking for the right words, I'll talk about inverse proportions some more. So like I said, the graph of an inverse proportion looks like this, and this shape is called a hyperbola."

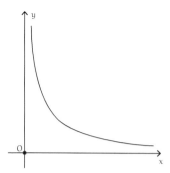

Graph of an inverse proportion (a hyperbola)

Yuri   "I guess that's a lot of what's bothering me. Proportions
         and inverse proportions feel like opposite things, so it
         seems like their graphs should be opposites too. And the
         opposite of a line that goes up is one that goes down.
         But these graphs aren't opposite, they're just different."

Me   "I see where you're coming from, but that's not the way
         to look at this. The graph of $y = ax$ goes up when $a > 0$,
         and down when $a < 0$. In other words, the only difference
         is if a is positive or negative. But that doesn't change
         anything about the original relationship, $y = ax$."

Yuri   "Aha, positive and negative. There's the 'opposite' I was
         looking for."

Me   "There you go. Let's write that down so we don't forget
         it."

---

a in the graph of $y = ax$

- When the line goes up, a is positive, and y increases when
  x increases.

- When the line goes down, a is negative, and y decreases
  when x increases.

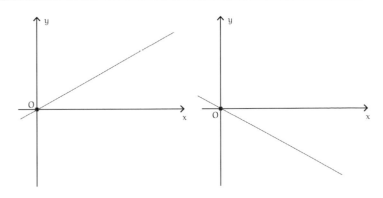

Graph with $a > 0$ (left) and $a < 0$ (right)

Me   "But $y = \dfrac{a}{x}$ is a completely different equation, so it's no surprise that its shape is completely different, too."

Yuri   "Well *I* was surprised."

Me   "Again, no surprise."

Yuri   "Very funny. So what about that other shape? A hyper something?"

Me   "A hyperbola."

Yuri   "That's the one. I'm still not convinced that thing is the opposite of a straight line."

Me   "Let's play with the form of the equation and see what we can find. Maybe we'll stumble across the opposites you're looking for."

4.7 CHANGING THE FORM OF EQUATIONS

Me   "Start with the equation for a proportion. We'll assume that x isn't 0."

$$y = ax \quad \text{equation of a proportion}$$
$$y \div x = a \quad \text{divide both sides by x (which isn't 0)}$$

Yuri   "What's the big deal? All you did was divide y by x."

Me   "And look at what that gave us, this new equation $y \div x = a$. Stare at that for a minute and tell me what you're able to read from the equation."

Yuri   "Staring...Staring..."

A problem

What can you read from this form of the equation for a proportion?

$$y \div x = a$$

Me   "Whatcha find?"

Yuri   "Not a thing."

Me   "How about the fact that a is constant? So if y is proportional to x, then $y \div x$ is a constant value, right?"

Yuri   "All 'constant' means is that it doesn't change, right?"

Me   "Well, yeah, but that's saying a lot. Variables like x and y are supposed to be able to take any value, but here you're saying that they can't."

Yuri   "Wait, I'm saying what?"

Me   "When you say that $y \div x$ has to equal some constant value a, you're creating a constraint on what x and y can be."

Yuri   "A constraint."

Me   "Right. Those variables can still take various values, but not just anything. You've *constrained* them as to what they can be. The constraint is that when y is proportional to x, dividing y by x always has to give you some specific value, a."

Answer

In a proportion, $y \div x$ is a constant

$$y \div x = a \quad \text{(a constant)}$$

Me   "Now, back to inverse proportions."

Yuri   "It's about time!"

Me   "Start by changing the form of the equation again. Remember the equation for an inverse proportion?"

Yuri   "Yup. $y = \dfrac{a}{x}$."

Me   "Which means we can also write it like this."

$$y = \frac{a}{x} \qquad \text{inverse proportion equation}$$
$$y \times x = a \qquad \text{multiply both sides by } x$$

Me   "What did I do?"

Yuri   "It's multiplication now."

Me   "Right. Now stare at this one and tell me what you see."

A Problem

What can you read from this form of the inverse proportion equation?
$$y \times x = a$$

Yuri   "No need for staring this time. The multiplication is a constant!

Me   "Bingo."

Answer

In an inverse proportion, $y \times x$ is a constant

$$y \times x = a \quad \text{(a constant)}$$

Me   "So now we're saying that if y is inversely proportional to x, then $y \times x$ has to be a constant value. Let's summarize what we've covered so far. Assuming that $x \neq 0 \ldots$"

Proportions and inverse proportions

If proportional . . . $y \div x = a$ (a constant)

If inversely proportional . . . $y \times x = a$ (a constant)

Me   "Now do you see the opposites you wanted?"

Yuri   "Hey, yeah! Multiplication and division! That's pretty opposite! And I guess this is another one of those constraints?"

Me   "Sure. The opposite kind of constraint, if you want to look at it that way."

Yuri   "Phew!"

Sunlight flashes off of Yuri's chestnut hair as she looks back and forth between the graphs.

Me   "While we're at it, you can also call $y \div x$ the ratio of y and x."

Yuri   "That sounds familiar, but it doesn't look it."

Me   "You may have seen ratios written as $y : x$. The value of that ratio is defined as what you get when you divide the numbers. So be careful when you talk about ratios;

you have to assume that x and y aren't 0. But anyway, when you say that x is proportional to y, you're saying that the value of their ratio is a constant."

Yuri   "Got it."

Me   "Good. So, moving on—"

Yuri   "Hold up, one thing I'm not clear on."

Me   "Ask away."

Yuri   "So, I get it that proportional numbers give a constant when you divide them, and inversely proportional numbers give a constant when you multiply them, but..."

Me   "But what?"

Yuri   "Mmm...not sure how to put this. It's like, where's the constant in the graphs?"

Me   "I'm not sure I see what you mean."

Yuri   "I don't think I said it right. I guess what I'm not seeing is why division being constant gives you a straight line, but multiplication being constant give you a hyperbola."

Me   "Ah, good point. I'm not sure how well I can answer that, but maybe looking at the relation between constraints and the shapes of graphs will clear things up."

4.8 What's the a in the Graph of a Proportion?

Yuri's question about proportions

Q: If $y \div x$ is a constant, why is its graph a straight line?

Me   "So the equation for a proportion was $y = ax$, right? Do you see what a is in the graph?"

A problem

In the proportion equation $y = ax$, what is a in the graph?

Yuri   "This sounds awfully familiar, but it isn't coming back to me."

Me   "I think *slope* is the word you're looking for. In the equation $y = ax$, the bigger a is, the steeper the line becomes."

Yuri   "Slope, right, that's it."

Me   "It's a graphing term you probably learned when you first started studying graphs. Something about 'when you move one to the right, you move up by the slope'? That's this a here."

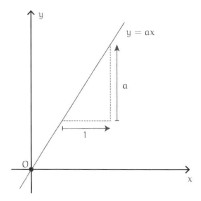

When you move 1 to the right, you move up (or down) by a.

Yuri   "A graphing term, huh."

Me   "Well, that's what I call it, since I doubt you use it much anywhere else."

> **Answer**
>
> In the proportion equation $y = ax$, the a is the slope of the graph.

Me   "If you wanted to put it in terms of an equation, I guess you'd say 'every time x increases by 1, y increases by a.'"

Yuri   "So if a gets crazy big, so does y!"

Me   "If $a > 0$, at least. Yeah, then the graph will shoot up. Anyway, we have the proportion equation as $y = ax$, with a as a constant that tells you which way the graph will move. So do you see how a being constant means the slope has to be constant too?"

Yuri   "I guess it would mean that, yeah."

Me   "Carrying that a step further, this means that having a constant slope is a feature of *all* graphs of proportions. And what kind of graph has a constant slope?"

Yuri   "I believe that would be a straight line."

Me   "And now we understand the features of a proportion."

Yuri   "Case closed."

> **Answer to Yuri's question about proportions**
>
> Q: If $y \div x$ is a constant, why is its graph a straight line?
> A: Because the graph's slope must be constant, too.

4.9 What's the a in the Graph of an Inverse Proportion?

Me   "Let's do the same thing to inverse proportions and see what we find. The equation for an inverse proportions was $y = \dfrac{a}{x}$, right?"

Yuri   "Yep. Which means that $y \times x$ is a constant."

Yuri's question about inverse proportions

Q: If $y \times x$ is a constant, why is its graph a hyperbola?

Me   "With proportions, a gave the slope of the graph. So what do you think a represents in $y = \dfrac{a}{x}$?"

A problem

In the inverse proportion equation $y = \dfrac{a}{x}$, what does a tell you about the graph?

Me   "Actually, rather than 'represent,' maybe it's better to ask where the a shows up in the graph."

Yuri   "Meaning?"

Me   "It's a hint. Since $y \times x = a$, think about where $y \times x$ is in this graph."

Yuri   "Seriously, I have no idea."

Me   "Start by thinking of '$y \times x$' as 'vertical $\times$ horizontal.' Then a represents the area of a rectangle on the graph."

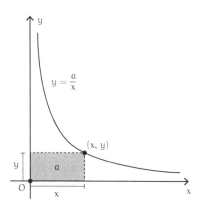

a is the area of a box with width x and height y.

Yuri   "Oh coool! At least, I guess that's cool. Wait, what's cool about this?"

Me   "Well, it's not so much cool as something to be aware of. Saying $y \times x = a$ implies that a is equivalent to the area of an x by y rectangle. That's the constraint that's drawing the hyperbola in the graph."

Yuri   "Because the area is fixed?"

Me   "Right. Pick any point on the curve, and a rectangle drawn between it and the origin will always have area a."

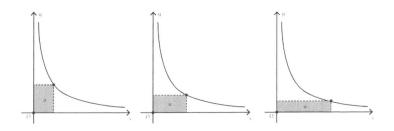

Yuri   "Ah, and the constant area is why moving the point farther off towards the edges makes the rectangle so narrow."

> **Answer**
>
> In the inverse proportion equation $y = \dfrac{a}{x}$, a is the area of the rectangle formed between a point on the curve and the origin.

Me   "That's right. So while a straight line is telling you that a slope is constant, the hyperbola is telling you that an area is constant."

Answer to Yuri's question about inverse proportions

Q: If $y \times x$ is a constant, why is its graph a hyperbola?

A: Because a rectangle drawn between a point on the curve and the origin must have a constant area.

Yuri looks back and forth between the graph and the equation.

Yuri   "Okay, you win. Jumping back and forth between graphs and equations like that is kinda cool."

Me   "I agree. It's neat to make those little changes, and make discoveries like fixed values for multiplication and division."

Yuri   "Playing with the graphs is even cooler."

I was struck by a thought. Had I really answered Yuri's question? I thought I nailed the part about straight lines, but the hyperbolas? Restrictions on the area of a rectangle are what created that curve. But was that really all? Had I missed something?

Me   "Hey, Yuri, I was just thinking . . ."

Mom   "Anybody want cookies?"

Yuri   "I never don't want cookies! C'mon, let's eat!"

Me   "Yeah. Yeah, sure."

Yuri yanks my arm. Nothing shuts down math talk like a summons from the kitchen.

Later I reflected on how proportions and inverse proportions were yet another one of those things I thought I understood so well, yet couldn't quite put into words.

I also noticed something. While their personalities were as different as night and day, Yuri and Tetra had one thing in common: they knew what they didn't know and weren't afraid to admit it.

"...and problem solvers never overlook a lack of change."

Problems for Chapter 4

Problem 4-1 (Area of a square)

Is there a proportional relation between the area of a square and the length of its sides?

(Answer on page 142)

Problem 4-2 (Equations of proportions)

Find the equations in which y is proportional to x:

1. $y = 3x$

2. $y = 3x + 1$

3. $3y = x$

4. $y - 3x = 0$

(Answer on page 142)

Problem 4-3 (Exchanging x and y)

If y is proportional to x, can you also say that x is proportional to y?

(Answer on page 143)

Problem 4-4 (Constant sums)

This conversation discussed two types of constant values for a, one where $y \div x = a$ and one where $y \times x = a$. If instead you have $y + x = a$, what kind of graph would that describe?

(Answer on page 143)

Problem 4-5 (Lines through the origin)

On page 74, the narrator makes two claims:

1. That any graph of a proportion will go through the origin.

2. That any graph that's a straight line going through the origin will be the graph of a proportion.

His first claim is correct, but the second one isn't always. Why not?

(Answer on page 144)

CHAPTER 5

Intersections and Tangents

"Without logic, there are no problem solvers..."

5.1 IN THE LIBRARY

I went to the library after school and found Tetra at our usual table, arms folded deep in thought. She didn't seem to notice me until I sat down next to her.

Tetra   "Gyaaaah!"

Me   "Whoa!"

          Everyone in the library looks at us, including Ms. Mizutani, who's sorting books.

Tetra   "Wow, sorry. I didn't see you walk up."

Me   "My fault. I didn't mean to scare you. What's that you're so deep into?"

Tetra   "Remember the other day, when you were moving graphs around?"

Me   "Sure, we were playing with $y = x^2$, right?"

Tetra   "Exactly. To make a parabola that intersects the x-axis at $x = 0$ and $x = 2$, you used the quadratic $(x-0)(x-2)$."

Me   "Right. $(x - 0)(x - 2) = x^2 - 2x$, so the parabola is $y = x^2 - 2x$."

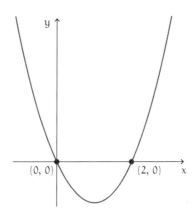

The parabola $y = x^2 - 2x$ crosses the x-axis where $x = 0$ and $x = 2$.

Tetra   "Yeah, but ..."

Me   "Does something look wrong?"

Tetra   "It's not that. I'm sure everything you did was right, it's just ... I don't know, I still feel like I don't get it. Not completely."

Me   "And you don't want to move on until you're sure you *do* get it. Nothing wrong with that. It's a great attitude to have, even."

Tetra   "Maybe, yeah, but it's kind of embarrassing. I mean, this is stuff we studied back in middle school."

Me   "*When* you studied something doesn't have much to do with how well you learned it. And like you say, the important thing is that feeling that you really understand it."

Tetra	"Yeah, you're right. I guess I'll just keep at it, then."
Me	"I'd be happy to help, if you like."
Tetra	"That would be great!"
Me	"Where do you want to begin?"
Tetra	"Uh ... from the very beginning."

5.2 THE x-AXIS

Me   "From the very beginning, then: the x-axis in a coordinate plane. First, tell me what you know about the x-axis"

A problem

Describe the x-axis.

Tetra   "Hmm, let's see. The x-axis is a line, and it goes through the origin, and it's, um, horizontal? Is that what you're looking for?"

Me   "Sure, that's good for now. You're definitely right about it being a straight line that goes through the origin. And it's often used as the horizontal axis, so calling it 'horizontal' isn't wrong, I guess. But let's try to really pin the thing down. What can you tell me about a point (x, y) that's on the x-axis?"

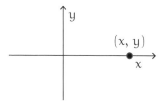

A point (x, y) on the x-axis.

Tetra   "Well, uh...I guess y will always be 0, right?"

Me   "Sure, that's a very important property. To be a little bit picky, though, it might be better to say 'y *is equal to* 0,' not 'y *is* 0."

Tetra   "Okay, then y *is equal* to 0."

Me   "Since we know that, do you see how in this case we can always write $(x, 0)$ instead of just (x, y)?"

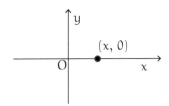

You can also write $(x, 0)$ for a point on the x-axis.

Tetra   "I see that, sure."

Me   "So we can say that if a point (x, y) is on the x-axis, then $y = 0$. We can also flip that around and say that if $y = 0$, then a point (x, y) is on the x-axis."

Tetra   "Uh...okay. No wait. Not okay."

          Tetra raises her hand.

Me   "Something bugging you?"

Tetra   "I think I got lost with the flipping around. What did you do there?"

Me   "Ah, right, let's be a bit more precise. Given what we've said so far, this proposition holds for a point (x, y) in a coordinate plane."

Proposition 1

▷ Point (x, y) is on the x-axis $\implies y = 0$

Tetra   "Okay, sure."

Me   "The 'flipping around' I was talking about means flipping the direction of this arrow to create Proposition 2. You read that arrow as 'implies.'"

Proposition 2

▷ Point (x, y) is on the x-axis $\impliedby y = 0$

Tetra   "So writing it backwards like this is like saying '$y = 0$ implies that point (x, y) is on the x-axis,' right?"

Me   "Exactly. To use the math term, we can say that Proposition 2 is the converse of Proposition 1, and Proposition 1 is the converse of Proposition 2."

Tetra   "The 'converse.' Got it."

Tetra jots this down in her notebook.

Me   "One more thing: when both $P \Rightarrow Q$ and $P \Leftarrow Q$ are true, you can say 'P if and only if Q.' Sometimes you'll see that abbreviated as 'P iff Q.'"

Tetra   "P? Q? Where did they come from?"

Me   "Using Proposition 1 as an example, P would be the condition 'point (x, y) is on the x-axis,' and Q would be the condition '$y = 0$.'"

Tetra   "Okay ..."

Me   "We're getting off track a little. Let's get back to our propositions."

Propositions 1 and 2

Proposition 1:

▷ Point (x, y) is on the x-axis $\implies$ $y = 0$

Proposition 2:

▷ Point (x, y) is on the x-axis $\impliedby$ $y = 0$

Me   "Both of these are true statements, so we can make a third proposition, using the double arrow symbol to indicate an if-and-only-if relation."

Proposition 3

Proposition 3:

▷ Point (x, y) is on the x-axis $\iff$ $y = 0$

Tetra   "So you're saying that the conditions 'point (x, y) is on the x-axis' and '$y = 0$' are the same thing?"

Me   "Sort of. But to introduce another math term, rather than 'the same thing,' let's say they're 'equivalent.'"

Tetra   "Isn't 'equivalent' the same thing as the same thing? Er, I mean, isn't 'the same thing' equivalent to 'equivalent'? No, wait, I meant to say—argh!"

Tetra holds her head in her hands.

Me   "Never mind, let's get back to talking about the x-axis. Like we said, in the coordinate plane, 'point (x, y) is on the x-axis' and '$y = 0$' are equivalent statements. So, for example, if you want to know if point (x, y) is on the x-axis, you just have to check if y equals 0."

Tetra   "Yeah . . . right."

Me	"Are you sure you're following this?"
Tetra	"Well, I get it, but I don't think I *get* it. There seem to be too many obvious things to keep track of."
Me	"Maybe it will be easier if you keep in mind that we're trying to tie together the world of graphs and the world of equations."
Tetra	"How's that?"
Me	"Well, asking if a point is on the x-axis is a question related to graphs, right?"
Tetra	"Because points are graphy things?"
Me	"Right. And doesn't $y = 0$ feel like something from the world of equations?"
Tetra	"Oh, I see! And saying they're equivalent brings together graphs with equations! Neat! Hang on, I want to write this down."

Tetra writes furtively in her notebook.

5.3 SPEAKING OF PARABOLAS

Me	"Okay, I think we're good with the x-axis stuff. We agree that 'point (x, y) is on the x-axis' and '$y = 0$' are equivalent statements. That means you could also say that the x-axis is the line that fulfills the condition $y = 0$."

Answer

The x-axis is the line that fulfills the condition $y = 0$.

Tetra	"Got it!"
Me	"Okay, then let's move on to parabolas. We'll use the parabola described by the equation $y = x^2 - 2x$ as an example. That one looks like this."

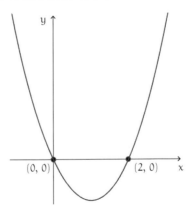

The parabola represented by $y = x^2 - 2x$.

Tetra's hand shoots up.

Me   "You have a question?"

Tetra   "Sorry to keep interrupting, but . . . you just used the word 'equation,' right?"

Me   "Sure, I said that the equation of this parabola is $y = x^2 - 2x$. Something wrong?"

Tetra   "This is probably just me being dumb, but when I hear the word 'equation,' it makes me think I'm supposed to solve for x. At least, that's what it usually means at school. But a parabola is a kind of graph, right? So how can it also be an equation? We aren't supposed to, like, solve it or anything, are we?"

Me   "That isn't dumb at all. I'm glad you're paying attention to the words we use. But maybe it's easier if we just forget about the word 'equation' for a minute. It's better to think of $y = x^2 - 2x$ as being a statement, one that describes the relationship between x and y. It says that if $x = 1$, then y must equal -1, right? So long as x is 1, y can never be 2 or 3 or whatever."

Tetra   "And you get that from plugging a 1 into the x's, and working it out, right?"

$$y = x^2 - 2x \qquad \text{equation of a parabola}$$
$$= 1^2 - 2 \times 1 \qquad \text{for example, substitute } x = 1$$
$$= 1 - 2 \qquad \text{because } 1^2 = 1$$
$$= -1 \qquad \text{because } 1 - 2 = -1$$

Me   "Sure, you've got it. This means if we're going to say that $y = x^2 - 2x$, then when $x = 1$ it must be true that $y = -1$. That's the relationship between x and y that the statement $y = x^2 - 2x$ is describing."

Tetra   "Okay, I see."

Me   "And do you also see that saying 'when $x = 1$, $y = -1$' is a description from the world of equations?"

Tetra   "Oh, yeah!"

Me   "And that for this parabola, x and y can't just take any value they want? That they have to work together, to fulfill the condition $y = x^2 - 2x$?"

Tetra   "Yep! It's like a rule that they have to obey."

Me   "Sure, you could call it a rule. A rule created by the parabola $y = x^2 - 2x$."

I realized that something similar had come up with Yuri when we were talking about 'constraints.'

Me   "Let's also take a closer look at the coordinate plane. Do you see how x and y can be any real number you want, and how there will always be a single point somewhere in the coordinate plane that corresponds to (x, y)?"

Tetra   "Corresponds... Yeah, sure."

| Me | "And since we can let x and y be any real number we want, we can move that point (x, y) anywhere on the coordinate plane that we want to. *But ...*" |

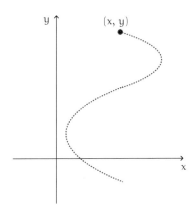

A point (x, y) can move freely in the coordinate plane.

| Tetra | "But?" |

| Me | "But what happens if we have this rule that says $y = x^2 - 2x$? Can our point move anywhere it wants, if it's going to obey that rule?" |

| Tetra | "I ... don't think so?" |

| Me | "Right. The point (x, y) is restricted as to where it can go. Now there are places where that point can be, and places where it can't. Do you see where the point can exist?" |

| Tetra | "Oh! It has to be on the parabola!" |

| Me | "Exactly. The rule $y = x^2 - 2x$ is a limit on where (x, y) is allowed to go. And if you look at all the places where it's allowed to go, all at the same time, then that forms a graph—a graph of a parabola." |

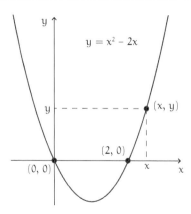

This parabola is formed from all the places where point (x, y) can go and still fulfill the condition that $y = x^2 - 2x$.

Tetra   "There it is!"

Me   "So let's get back to that word 'equations.' When you 'solve' an equation, what you're doing is finding all of the values for x or y or whatever unknown variables are in it that make the statement true."

Tetra   "Right."

Me   "And when you graph this parabola, you're drawing all the points (x, y) that have x and y values that make $y = x^2 - 2x$ true."

Tetra   "Yeah, sure."

Me   "So if you think about it, isn't *graphing* the parabola sorta the same thing as *solving* the equation $y = x^2 - 2x$? After all, if a point (x, y) is on the parabola, then x and y fulfill the condition that $y = x^2 - 2x$."

Tetra   "And vice-versa!"

Me   "Right. If x and y fulfill the condition that $y = x^2 - 2x$..."

Tetra   "Then the point (x, y) is on the parabola!"

Me   "And that means that saying 'the point (x, y) is on the parabola $y = x^2 - 2x$' and saying 'x and y fulfill the condition $y = x^2 - 2x$' are...?"

Tetra   "Equivalent statements!"

Me   "Bingo. And that's why we can say that *graphing* the parabola is in a sense the same as *solving* the equation. So now do you see why saying 'the equation of a parabola' makes sense?"

Tetra   "I do!"

            Tetra jots down more notes.

Tetra   "This is another example of tying together the world of graphs and the world of equations, isn't it! Like when we talked about the x-axis and $y = 0$."

The world of graphs	The world of equations
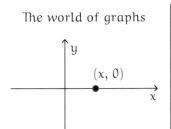	$y = 0$

Me   "Yeah, it is, isn't it."

Tetra   "And now we're tying together parabolas with $y = x^2 - 2x$."

The world of graphs	The world of equations
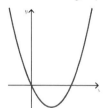	$y = x^2 - 2x$

Me   "Good for you, seeing the connection. You're a quick learner."

Tetra   "Nah, I'm just a good note-taker."

           Tetra covers her face with the notebook, but I can still see her blush.

5.4 Intersecting Points

Me   "Let's move on to something new: points of intersection."

Tetra   "You bet!"

Me   "The points of intersection between a parabola and the x-axis will be the places where the two meet."

Tetra   "Right."

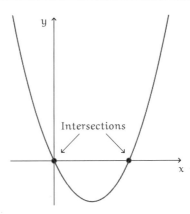

A parabola and its intersections with the x-axis.

Me   "Talking about points of intersection is something out of
            the world of graphs, right? But when—"

Miruka   "You two look like you're having fun."

Tetra   "Hey, Miruka!"

Me   "We're talking about parabolas and the x-axis."

Miruka   "Oh yeah?"

Miruka pushes her glasses further up her nose.

Tetra   "Yeah, because I'm all confused about moving parabolas
            around."

Miruka   "Quadratic equations, huh?"

Me   "Yeah, we're heading there, at least."

Miruka   "Well don't let me stop you."

Miruka takes a seat across from us and begins
reading a book.

Me   "You know that there are infinitely many points on the
            parabola $y = x^2 - 2x$, right?"

Tetra	"Sounds familiar, yeah."

Tetra traces a parabola in the air.

Me	"And we've talked about how there's a rule that x and y have to follow to be on the parabola."

Tetra	"Sure, they have to make $y = x^2 - 2x$ be a true statement."

Me	"That's also true for the x-axis, right? It's a collection of infinitely many points, and every one of them has to obey another rule."

Tetra	"Yep. Their rule is that y has to be 0, and x ... well, I guess x doesn't really have a rule."

Me	"That's right, it doesn't. So now we want to think about the points that will be on both the parabola and the x-axis. Those are the points of intersection."

Tetra	"Sure! These points here, right?"

Me	"Yep, those are the ones. Now these points have their own rule."

Tetra	"A special rule for intersections? Hmm, let's see. Uh..."

Tetra scowls and mumbles to herself.

Me	"You're probably thinking too much. Just remember what we said about parabolas and the x-axis."

The parabola

World of Graphs		World of Equations
Point (x, y) is on parabola $y = x^2 - 2x$	$\iff$	$y = x^2 - 2x$

The x-axis

World of Graphs		World of Equations
Point (x, y) is on the x-axis	$\Longleftrightarrow$	$y = 0$

Tetra   "Okay."

Me   "So here's the problem. It's pretty easy to make a statement from the world of graphs, like this: 'The point (x, y) is on both the parabola $y = x^2 - 2x$ and the x-axis.' But how can we say the same thing, using a statement from the world of equations?"

The worlds of graphs and equations

World of Graphs		World of Equations
Point (x, y) is an intersection between the parabola $y = x^2 - 2x$ and the x-axis.	$\Longleftrightarrow$	???

Tetra begins an animated attempt at an explanation.

Tetra   "So the intersection between two graphs is, uh, where they cross, right? And where they cross is a point, so... Wow, it's hard to put into words."

Me   "Don't worry, giving a good description of a point of intersection isn't as easy as it might seem."

Tetra   "But it's like...I know what I want to say, I just don't know how to say it."

Me   "How about if we reword things like this?"

Rewording the problem

Point (x, y) is an intersection between the parabola $y = x^2 - 2x$ and the x-axis.

Tetra   "That's different?"

Me   "A little. We can even take it a step further."

Rewording the problem

The point (x, y) is on the parabola $y = x^2 - 2x$, and it's also on the x-axis.

Tetra   "So you're saying that the point is on both at the same time?"

Me   "Right, it's a point on both of the graphs. That's exactly what it means to be an intersection."

Tetra   "Well, yeah, it is, but maybe I'm missing the point."

Me   "That might be because we're still stuck in the world of graphs."

           Miruka suddenly joins in.

Miruka   "The world of graphs?"

Me   "Yeah, I've been explaining things in terms of being in the world of graphs or the world of equations."

Miruka   "Hmph. Sounds like you need to take things up a notch.
            She's smarter than you're giving her credit for."

            Miruka returns to her book.

Me   "Anyway, let's think about what goes here, in place of
            these question marks that correspond to being on both
            graphs."

Problem

What goes in place of the question marks?

World of Graphs   **World of Equations**

Point (x, y) is on
both the parabola
$y = x^2 - 2x$ and $\Longleftrightarrow$???
the x-axis.

Tetra   "Hmm, let's see ..."

Me   "Try thinking about how you can make both $y = x^2 - 2x$
            and $y = 0$ true."

Tetra   "Make *both* of them true?"

Me   "Sure. That's what we want to do, right? Fulfill the con-
            ditions for both the equation of the parabola and equa-
            tion for the x-axis."

Answer

World of Graphs		World of Equations
Point (x, y) is on both the parabola $y = x^2 - 2x$ and the x-axis.	$\Longleftrightarrow$	For x and y, both $y = x^2 - 2x$ and $y = 0$ are true statements.

Tetra   "Oh, sure. Of course."

Me   "So what we're saying is that a point of intersection has to make two equations both true statements."

Tetra   "Right."

Miruka glances up at me. She looks like she has something she wants to say.

Me   "So where are we now?"

Tetra   "What do you mean?"

Me   "Well, we've reached a place that we should know well."

Tetra   "A place we know well?"

Tetra looks around the room.

Me   "Sure. We want to find points that make two equations both true. At the same time. *Simultaneously*. As in—"

Tetra   "Simultaneous equations!"

Me   "There ya go."

$$\begin{cases} y = x^2 - 2x & \cdots \text{(a) equation of a parabola} \\ y = 0 & \cdots \text{(b) equation of the x-axis} \end{cases}$$

Tetra   "You're right! I've done this before!"

Me   "Sure you have. If you want to find x and y values that
             make two equations both true, then you just have to
             solve the system of equations. That's exactly the method
             to use when you want to find points that are the inter-
             section between two graphs: just set the equations for
             those graphs into a system of equations."

Tetra   "That makes so much sense!"

Finding intersections between two graphs

Solve the equations for the graphs as a system of equations.

Me   "Let's do that for these equations (a) and (b)."

$$\begin{cases} y & = x^2 - 2x \qquad \cdots \text{(a) equation of a parabola} \\ y & = 0 \qquad\qquad \cdots \text{(b) equation of the x-axis} \end{cases}$$

$$
\begin{array}{rcll}
0 & = & x^2 - 2x & \text{substitute (b), } y = 0, \text{ into (a)} \\
x^2 - 2x & = & 0 & \text{swap sides} \\
x(x - 2) & = & 0 & \text{factor out an x}
\end{array}
$$

Me   "Since $x(x - 2)$ equals 0, that means either $x = 0$ or
             $x = 2$. And since (b) says that $y = 0$, we have two points
             of intersection: $(x, y) = (0, 0)$ and $(x, y) = (2, 0)$."

Finding points of intersection

Find the points of intersection between the parabola $y = x^2 - 2x$ and the x-axis by solving the following system of equations:

$$\begin{cases} y & = x^2 - 2x \\ y & = 0 \end{cases}$$

The points of intersection are thus $(x, y) = (0, 0), (2, 0)$.

Tetra stares at what I've written.

Tetra   "Okay, I think I've got it. It goes like this."

> We want to find the point of intersection between a parabola and the x-axis.

> We need to find the points that make the equations for the parabola and the x-axis both true.

> We set the two equations up as a system of equations, and solve.

Me   "That's exactly right. Good summary. Add to that the fact that finding the points of intersection between a parabola and the x—axis is the same thing as solving the quadratic equation for the parabola when $y = 0$."

- $y = x^2 - 2x$ is the equation for a parabola.

- When $y = 0$, we have the quadratic $0 = x^2 - 2x$.

Tetra   "Oh, right. $x^2 - 2x = 0$ is a quadratic, isn't it."

Me   "Right. And you can easily solve it by factoring out an x."

Tetra   "When we did it this time, you wrote that as $x(x-2)$, but didn't you do the same thing the other day as $(x-0)(x-2)$?"

Me   "You're right, I did. Either way is fine, of course, but I think it's easier to see the x-coordinates when you write it out like that. See how the 0 and the 2 kind of pop out at you?"

$$(x - \underline{0})(x - \underline{2}) = 0$$

Tetra   "It's so neat how all these different kinds of equations are all related. The equation for a parabola, quadratic equations, second degree equations, factored equations..."

5.5 Tangent Points

Miruka snaps her book shut.

Miruka   "I'm going to go crazy if you don't hurry up and get to tangents."

Me   "Huh?"

Miruka   "And at least move the parabola around a little. How about using $y = x^2 - 2x + 1$ instead. What points are on the parabola and the x-axis now?"

Miruka jabs a finger straight at me.

Me   "Well, now we just set $y = x^2 - 2x + 1$ and $y = 0$ as a system of equations, so I guess the answer is $(1, 0)$. Ah, that's a tangent point, isn't it."

Tetra   "Whoa, how did you figure that out without graphing anything?"

Me   "Just look at the form of the equation $y = x^2 - 2x + 1$."

Tetra   "The form of the equation?"

Me   "Do you see how you would factor that?"

$$x^2 - 2x + 1 = (x - 1)^2$$

Tetra   "Yeah, so?"

Me   "Well, when we rewrite Miruka's parabola as $(x - 1)^2$
          we have x captured inside that square, right? Maybe
          you've heard of this as something called 'completing the
          square.'"

$y = x^2 - 2x + 1$ equation of a parabola

$y = (x - 1)^2$ complete the square

Tetra   "Sounds familiar."

Me   "So when we solve this system of equations . . ."

$$\begin{cases} y = (x - 1)^2 & \cdots \text{equation of a parabola} \\ y = 0 & \cdots \text{equation of the x-axis} \end{cases}$$

Me   ". . . we get the point $(x, y) = (1, 0)$."

Tetra   "And you said that's a tangent point?"

Me   "Right."

Miruka   "Completing the square and all that is fine, but maybe
          it would be helpful to draw a graph?"

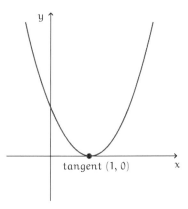

The parabola $y = x^2 - 2x + 1$

Tetra   "I see! The parabola doesn't *cross* the x-axis, it's more
           like it just *touches* it. So that's what a tangent point
           is!"

Me   "Yeah. Before I said that solving the system of equations
           would give you intersections, but I should have men-
           tioned that you can get tangents, too."

Finding intersections or tangents between two graphs

Solve the equations for the graphs as a system of equations.

Two intersections

The parabola $y = x^2 - 2x$ intersects the x-axis at two points.

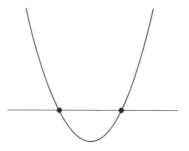

One intersection (tangent)

The parabola $y = x^2 - 2x + 1$ is **tangent** to the x-axis at one point.

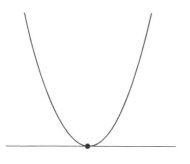

Tetra   "So intersections and tangents are different?"

Miruka   "It's not that simple, because the word 'intersect' is kind of fuzzy. Lots of textbooks treat tangent points as a kind of intersection, just one that happens when two graphs are touching."

Me   "Ah, interesting."

Miruka   "Then again, I seem to recall our high school math book
            saying they're different things. I've seen some books com-
            bine both into something called a 'common point,' but
            that term hasn't really caught on yet."

Tetra takes notes furiously.

Tetra   "A common point . . ."

Miruka   "In any case, the process of finding them is the same: set
            the two equations up as a system of equations and solve
            to find the intersections, or tangents, or whatever you
            want to call them."

Miruka pauses to give Tetra time to catch up.

Miruka   "Let's get back to those completed squares and do some
            graphing of $y = (x - 1)^2 + \alpha$. Five of them should be
            enough."

Draw the graph of equations (a) through (e)

$$y = (x - 1)^2 - 2 \qquad \text{(a)}$$
$$y = (x - 1)^2 - 1 \qquad \text{(b)}$$
$$y = (x - 1)^2 + 0 \qquad \text{(c)}$$
$$y = (x - 1)^2 + 1 \qquad \text{(d)}$$
$$y = (x - 1)^2 + 2 \qquad \text{(e)}$$

Miruka   "This isn't hard at all; just think of $y = (x - 1)^2 + \alpha$ as
            being the parabola $y = (x-1)^2$ raised up or down by α."

Me   "I see."

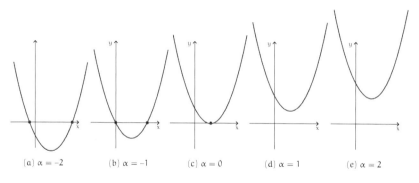

(a) $\alpha = -2$ (b) $\alpha = -1$ (c) $\alpha = 0$ (d) $\alpha = 1$ (e) $\alpha = 2$

Graphs of $y = (x - 1)^2 + \alpha$

Tetra   "Each one gets a little higher. And the intersections with the x-axis get closer and closer, until they meet in (c), where they become a tangent!"

Me   "Right."

Miruka   "Then what happens, starting with (d)?"

Miruka looks expectantly at Tetra.

Tetra   "Um, once you get past (c) the parabola leaves the x-axis behind. There aren't any intersections *or* tangents!"

Me   "Yeah, that's what you would say in the world of graphs. In the world of equations, you would say there's no solution."

Miruka   "No *real number* solution, you mean. Even if there are no common points in the coordinate plane, there can still be complex solutions."

Me   "Yep, you got me there."

Tetra   "Even if there are no common points, there can still be complex solutions. . ."

Me   "Something still not making sense, Tetra?"

Tetra   "Ignore me—I'm just thinking out loud."

Me   "If there's anything we can help you with—"

Tetra covers her face with her notebook.

Tetra   "No, no. I'm good for now."

Ms. Mizutani "The library is *closed*!"

And with that, our math talk came to an end. I wondered what was bothering Tetra, but I decided it might be best to give her some time to work things out on her own.

"...and there are no problem solvers who use only logic."

PROBLEMS FOR CHAPTER 5

Problem 5-1 (An equation for the y-axis)

The narrator and Tetra discussed an equation that represents the x-axis. Can you think of an equation that instead represents the y-axis?

(Answer on page 145)

Problem 5-2 (Intersections with the y-axis)

Where do the parabola $y = x^2 - 2x + 1$ and the y-axis intersect?

(Answer on page 145)

Problem 5-3 (Intersections of a parabola and a line)

Where do the parabola $y = x^2$ and the line $y = x$ intersect?

(Answer on page 146)

Epilogue

One day, in a quiet math department storeroom . . .

Girl   "Whoa, there's so much cool stuff in here!"

Teacher   "Yeah, it's fun to poke around."

Girl   "What's this?"

      The girl picks up an old handout.

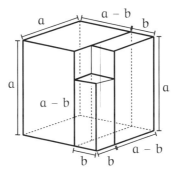

Teacher   "What do you think it is?"

Girl   "An identity?"

Teacher   "Very good. It's a graphical explanation of this identity."

$$(a - b)(a^2 + ab + b^2) = a^3 - b^3$$

Girl   "You'd expand that like this, right?"

$$(a - b)(a^2 + ab + b^2) = \underbrace{(a - b)a^2}_{\text{left solid}} + \underbrace{(a - b)ab}_{\text{right solid}} + \underbrace{(a - b)b^2}_{\text{center solid}}$$

$$= \underbrace{a^3}_{\text{large solid}} - \underbrace{b^3}_{\text{small removed solid}}$$

Teacher   "Very good."

Girl   "What's this?"

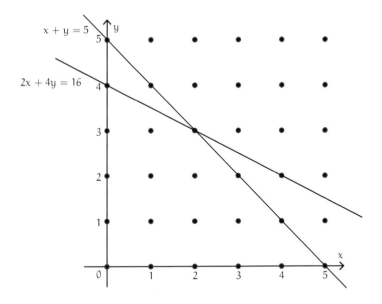

Teacher   "Any guesses?"

Girl   "Two lines. And lotsa dots."

Teacher   "It's a solution to a leg-counting problem."

Girl   "Leg counting?"

Teacher   "If you have a total of 5 cranes and turtles, and they have 16 legs among them, then how many cranes and how many turtles are there?"

Girl   "Isn't that a system of equations problem?"

$$\begin{cases} x + y & = 5 \\ 2x + 4y & = 16 \end{cases}$$

Teacher   "It is. And as it turns out, both $x+y = 5$ and $2x+4y = 16$ are both straight lines."

Girl   "So you're looking for where they intersect?"

Teacher   "That's right. When you solve the system of equations, you find they intersect at $(x, y) = (2, 3)$. You need to make sure that your answers are nonnegative integers, and that's what the dots are marking off."

Girl   "Hmm."

Teacher   "You see why (x, y) can't be just anything, right? Because you can't have a negative number of cranes or turtles—or partial ones, for that matter."

Girl   "So there's a limited set of answers."

Teacher   "A limit, a rule, a constraint . . . whatever you want to call it. In any case, the place where both lines cross at a point is your answer."

Girl   "So what's this?"

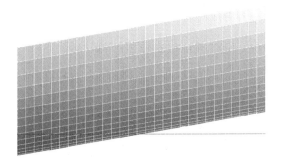

Teacher   "What do you think?"

Girl   "A parallelogram?"

Teacher   "Ah, I suppose it is, viewed from this angle."

Girl   "What do you mean, viewed from this angle?"

Teacher   "This is a three-dimensional object, seen from the side."

The teacher produces another piece of paper.

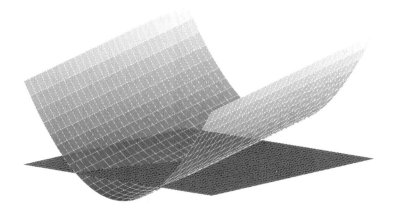

Teacher   "You make it by moving a parabola through space. See how it moves up as it goes back?"

Girl   "It looks like you're using a bent piece of paper to scoop up water."

Teacher   "When you move a point you get a curve. When you move a curve, you get a surface. It's basically the same thing, but taken up to three dimensions instead of two."

Girl   "Why would you want to do that?"

Teacher   "Well, you know how to use a two-dimensional graph to see the relationship between two things, right?"

Girl   "Like when we studied proportions and inverse proportions?"

Teacher   "Exactly. And if you use a three-dimensional graph, you can see the relationship between three things."

Girl   "Hard to draw a 3D graph on 2D paper, though."

Teacher   "Use a computer. Or your imagination."

Girl   "Imagination? In math?"

Teacher   "Sure. Imagine what the graph can become."

Girl   "If you say so."

Teacher   "We connect all kinds of worlds when we do math. The actual world and the mathematical world, the world of equations and the world of figures. We connect them by perceiving their structure. Doing that can feel like spreading your wings and flying."

Girl   "Now that you mention it, this graph looks kinda like a bird."

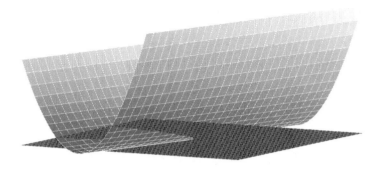

The girl laughs, waves, and flutters away.

Answers to Problems

Problem 1-1 (Expanding expressions)

Expand the following:

$$(x+y)^2$$

Answer 1-1 (Expanding expressions)
The following is an example of how this might be expanded:

$$
\begin{aligned}
(x+y)^2 &= (x+y)(x+y) & &(x+y)^2 \text{ means multiply two } (x+y)\text{'s} \\
&= (x+y)x + (x+y)y & &\text{multiply one } (x+y) \text{ through} \\
&= xx + yx + xy + yy & &\text{multiply x and y through} \\
&= x^2 + yx + xy + yy & &\text{xx is x squared} \\
&= x^2 + yx + xy + y^2 & &\text{yy is y squared} \\
&= x^2 + xy + xy + y^2 & &\text{yx and xy are equivalent} \\
&= x^2 + 2xy + y^2 & &\text{add the two xy's}
\end{aligned}
$$

Answer: $x^2 + 2xy + y^2$

Problem 1-2 (Calculating expressions)

Letting x be 3 and y be -2, calculate the following:

$$x^2 + 2xy + y^2$$

Answer 1-2 (substitute)

You can of course just substitute $x = 3, y = -2$ and solve like this:

$$
\begin{aligned}
x^2 + 2xy + y^2 &= 3^2 + 2 \cdot 3 \cdot (-2) + (-2)^2 \\
&= 9 - 12 + 4 \\
&= 1
\end{aligned}
$$

Answer: 1

But as we saw in Problem 1-1, $(x + y)^2 = x^2 + 2xy + y^2$. So $x^2 + 2xy + y^2$ and $(x + y)^2$ are equivalent, so we can use this to make the problem much simpler:

$$
\begin{aligned}
x^2 + 2xy + y^2 &= (x + y)^2 && \text{Identity} \\
&= (3 + (-2))^2 && \text{substitute } x = 3, y = -2 \\
&= (3 - 2)^2 && \text{remove the inner parentheses} \\
&= (1)^2 && \text{subtract} \\
&= 1 && \text{square 1}
\end{aligned}
$$

Answer: 1

Note that when you substitute the variables in an expression with numbers, the resulting calculation is called the value of the expression. So when $x = 3, y = -2$, the value of the expression $x^2 + 2xy + y^2$ is 1.

Problem 1-3 (Products of sums and differences)

Calculate the following:

$$202 \times 198$$

Answer 1-3 (Products of sums and differences)

Of course you can calculate this out the long way, but if you remember that "the product of a sum and a difference is a difference of squares," the calculation is easier, as follows:

$$
\begin{aligned}
202 \times 198 &= (200 + 2) \times (200 - 2) \\
&= 200^2 - 2^2 \qquad \text{product of a sum and a difference...} \\
&= 40000 - 4 \\
&= 39996
\end{aligned}
$$

<u>Answer: 39996</u>

ANSWERS TO CHAPTER 2 PROBLEMS

Problem 2-1 (Mathematical descriptions)

Use mathematical notation to represent the number of legs between x cranes and y turtles.

Answer 2-1 (Mathematical descriptions)

A crane has two legs, so if there are x cranes they must have $2x$ legs among them. Similarly, a turtle has four legs, so if there are y turtles there must be $4x$ turtle legs. So if you add those up, you have $2x + 4y$ legs all together.

Answer: $2x + 4y$ legs

Problem 2-2 (Mathematical descriptions)

Use mathematical notation to represent the number of legs between x animals that have a legs each, and y animals that have b legs each.

Answer 2-2 (Mathematical descriptions)

If there are x animals with a legs each, then together they must have ax legs. Similarly, if there are y animals with b legs each, then all together they will have by legs. The total must therefore be $ax + by$ legs.

Answer: $ax + by$ legs

Problem 2-3 (Solving systems of equations)

Solve the following system of equations:

$$\begin{cases} x + y = 6 \\ 2x + 3y = 14 \end{cases}$$

Answer 2-3 (Solving systems of equations)

$$\begin{cases} x + y = 6 & \cdots ① \\ 2x + 3y = 14 & \cdots ② \end{cases}$$

from $②-2\times①$

$$y = 2 \qquad\qquad \cdots ③$$

substitute $③$ into $①$

$$x + 2 = 6$$

subtract 2 from both sides

$$x = 6 - 2$$
$$= 4$$

Answer: $x = 4, y = 2$

Problem 2-4 (Solving systems of equations)

Solve the following system of equations:

$$\begin{cases} x + y = 99999 & \cdots ① \\ 2x + 4y = 375306 & \cdots ② \end{cases}$$

Answer 2-4 (Solving systems of equations)

$$\begin{cases} x + y & = 99999 & \cdots \text{(1)} \\ 2x + 4y & = 375306 & \cdots \text{(2)} \end{cases}$$

divide both sides of (2) by 2

$$x + 2y = 187653 \qquad\qquad \cdots \text{(3)}$$

from (3) − (1)

$$y = 87654 \qquad\qquad \cdots \text{(4)}$$

substitute (4) into (1)

$$x + 87654 = 99999$$

subtract 87654 from both sides

$$x = 99999 - 87654$$
$$= 12345$$

Answer: $x = 12345, y = 87654$

ANSWERS TO CHAPTER 3 PROBLEMS

Problem 3-1 (Writing polynomials)

Simplify the following expression, following the discussion on page 43:

$$1 + 2x + 3x^3 - 4x + 5x^2 + 6$$

Answer 3-1 (Writing polynomials)

$$1 + 2x + 3x^3 - 4x + 5x^2 + 6$$
$$= 1 - 2x + 3x^3 + 5x^2 + 6 \qquad \text{combine like terms } 2x \text{ and } -4x$$
$$= 7 - 2x + 3x^3 + 5x^2 \qquad \text{combine like terms } 1 \text{ and } 6$$
$$= 3x^3 + 5x^2 - 2x + 7 \qquad \text{rearrange in order of exponents}$$

Answer: $3x^3 + 5x^2 - 2x + 7$

Problem 3-2 (Writing polynomials)

Simplify the following expression, following the discussion on page 43:

$$1x^3 + 3x^1 - 5x^2 - 4x + 2x^2 + 2x^2$$

Be sure to pay attention to the following:

- Coefficients of 1 normally aren't written. (Example: $1x^3$ is normally written as x^3.)

- Exponents of 1 normally aren't written. (Example: $3x^1$ is normally written as $3x$.)

Answer 3-2 (Writing polynomials)

$$1x^3 + 3x^1 - 5x^2 - 4x + 2x^2 + 2x^2$$

$= x^3 + 3x^1 - 5x^2 - 4x + 2x^2 + 2x^2$	don't write coefficient 1
$= x^3 + 3x - 5x^2 - 4x + 2x^2 + 2x^2$	don't write exponent 1
$= x^3 - x - 5x^2 + 2x^2 + 2x^2$	combine like terms $3x$ and $-4x$
$= x^3 - x - x^2$	combine like terms $-5x^2$ and $2x^2$
$= x^3 - x^2 - x$	rearrange in order of exponents

Answer: $x^3 - x^2 - x$

Problem 3-3 (Degree of polynomials)

What is the degree of the following polynomial on x?

$$x^3 + x^2 - x^3 + x - 1$$

Answer 3-3 (Degree of polynomials)
Start by organizing this in the same manner as in the "Writing polynomials" problems.

$$x^3 + x^2 - x^3 + x - 1$$
$$= x^2 + x - 1 \qquad \text{combine like terms } x^3 \text{ and } -x^3 \text{ (giving 0)}$$

There are three terms in $x^2 + x - 1$: x^2, x, and -1. Of these, the term with the highest degree is x^2, which has degree 2. The degree of the given polynomial is thus 2.

Answer: 2nd degree

Problem 3-4 (Graphs of first degree functions)

Draw a graph of the following first degree function:

$$y = 2x - 4$$

Answer 3-4 (Graphs of first degree functions)

If we let $y = 0$, we have $0 = 2x - 4$, so $x = 2$, and we know that $(x, y) = (2, 0)$ is the intersection of the graph with the x-axis. When we let $x = 0$ we have that $y = -4$, so the intersection of the graph with the y-axis is $(0, -4)$. Drawing a line that passes through those points, we get something like this:

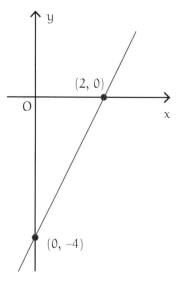

A graph of the 1st degree equation $y = 2x - 4$

Problem 3-5 (Graphs of second degree functions)

Draw a graph of the following second degree function:

$$y = -x^2 + 1$$

Answer 3-5 (Graphs of second degree functions)

Substituting $y = 0$ into $y = -x^2 + 1$, we get $0 = -x^2 + 1$. In other words, $x^2 - 1 = 0$. After factoring the left side this becomes $(x+1)(x-1) = 0$, so x is either 1 or -1. That means the intersections between this graph and the x-axis will be where the x-coordinate is 1 and -1.

When we substitute $x = 0$ into $y = -x^2 + 1$, we get $y = -0^2 + 1 = 1$, so $y = 1$. That means the intersection between this graph and the y-axis will be where the y-coordinate is 1.

Drawing the graph passing through these points on the x- and y-axes, we get a concave down parabola like this:

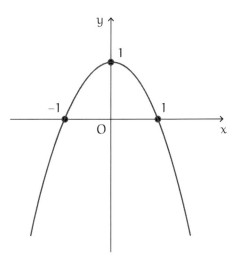

A graph of the 2nd degree equation $y = -x^2 + 1$ (Answer)

Note that when we compare the graphs of the second degree equations $y = -x^2 + 1$ and $y = x^2 - 1$, we see that the parabola flips across the x-axis:

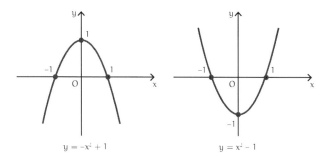

$$y = -x^2 + 1 \qquad y = x^2 - 1$$

This happens because multiplying $-x^2 + 1$ by -1 gives $x^2 - 1$ (and vice versa).

$$\boxed{-x^2 + 1} \xrightarrow{\text{multiply by } -1} \boxed{x^2 - 1}$$

Answers to Chapter 4 Problems

Problem 4-1 (Area of a square)

Is there a proportional relation between the area of a square and the length of its sides?

Answer 4-1 (Area of a square)

No, the relation between the area of a square and the length of its sides is not proportional. When the length of a square's sides doubles, its area quadruples. That's not a proportional relation.

To see this as an equation, let y be the area of a square, and let x be the length of its sides. Then the relation between x and y is $y = x^2$. This doesn't fall into the pattern of a proportional relation, which is $y = ax$.

Problem 4-2 (Equations of proportions)

Find the equations in which y is proportional to x:

1. $y = 3x$

2. $y = 3x + 1$

3. $3y = x$

4. $y - 3x = 0$

Answer 4-2 (Equations of proportions)

x and y are proportional in equations 1, 3, and 4. Let's look at each in turn:

1. $y = 3x$ perfectly follows the form of an equation of a proportion, $y = ax$.

2. There's no way to rearrange this into the form $y = ax$.

3. We can rearrange this by dividing both sides by 3, giving $y = \frac{1}{3}x$.

4. We can move the $-3x$ term to the right, giving $y = 3x$.

Problem 4-3 (Exchanging x and y)

If y is proportional to x, can you also say that x is proportional to y?

Answer 4-3 (Exchanging x and y)

Yes, if y is proportional to x, then x is proportional to y. This is because if y is proportional to x, then we can write their relation as $y = ax$, for some nonzero constant a. Next, we can divide both sides of $y = ax$ by a to rewrite the relation as $x = \frac{1}{a} \times y$.

Now let's rename $\frac{1}{a}$ as a', and rewrite this as $x = a'y$. This means that x is proportional to y. For example, when $y = 2x$, we have that $x = \frac{1}{2}y$.

Problem 4-4 (Constant sums)

This conversation discussed two types of constant values for a, one where $y \div x = a$ and one where $y \times x = a$. If instead you have $y + x = a$, what kind of graph would that describe?

Answer 4-4 (Constant sums)

Graphing $y + x = a$, we get something like this:

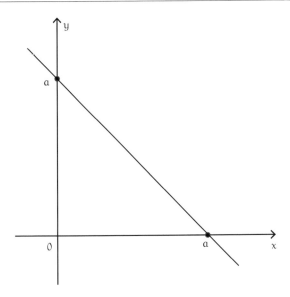

A graph of $y + x = a$

On page 126 there's an example of this when $a = 5$.

Problem 4-5 (Lines through the origin)

On page 74 the narrator makes two claims:

1. That any graph of a proportion will go through the origin.

2. That any graph that's a straight line going through the origin will be the graph of a proportion.

His first claim is correct, but the second one isn't always. Why not?

Answer 4-5 (Lines through the origin)

Not all straight lines that go through the origin will be the graph of a proportion, because there are two exceptions: the x-axis (the line $y = 0$) and the y-axis (the line $x = 0$) are both straight lines passing through the origin, but their equations do not describe x and y as being in a proportional relation.

ANSWERS TO CHAPTER 5 PROBLEMS

Problem 5-1 (An equation for the y-axis)

The narrator and Tetra discussed an equation that represents the x-axis. Can you think of an equation that instead represents the y-axis?

Answer 5-1 (An equation for the y-axis)
You can represent the straight line of the y-axis as $x = 0$.

$$\underline{\text{Answer: } x = 0}$$

Problem 5-2 (Intersections with the y-axis)

Where do the parabola $y = x^2 - 2x + 1$ and the y-axis intersect?

Answer 5-2 (Intersections with the y-axis)
To find this, solve the following system of equations:

$$\begin{cases} y & = x^2 - 2x + 1 \qquad \cdots \text{①} \text{ equation of the parabola} \\ x & = 0 \qquad\qquad\quad \cdots \text{②} \text{ equation of the y-axis} \end{cases}$$

Substitute ② into ①:

$$\begin{aligned} y &= 0^2 - 2 \cdot 0 + 1 \\ &= 1 \end{aligned}$$

The intersection we're after is therefore $(x, y) = (0, 1)$.

$$\underline{\text{Answer: } (x, y) = (0, 1)}$$

Problem 5-3 (Intersections of a parabola and a line)

Where do the parabola $y = x^2$ and the line $y = x$ intersect?

Answer 5-3 (Intersections of a parabola and a line)

To find this, solve the following system of equations:

$$\begin{cases} y &= x^2 \qquad \cdots \text{①} \ \text{equation of the parabola} \\ y &= x \qquad \cdots \text{②} \ \text{equation of the line} \end{cases}$$

Substitute $y = x$ from ② into the y of ①:

$$
\begin{aligned}
x &= x^2 \\
0 &= x^2 - x &&\text{move } x \text{ to the right} \\
x^2 - x &= 0 &&\text{exchange right and left sides} \\
x(x - 1) &= 0 &&\text{factor out an } x
\end{aligned}
$$

So we have either $x = 0$ or $x = 1$.

From ② we have that when $x = 0$, $y = 0$. From ② we also have that when $x = 1$, $y = 1$.

The point of intersection we're after is therefore $(x, y) = (0, 0), (1, 1)$.

Answer: $(x, y) = (0, 0), (1, 1)$

You can also confirm that visually using a graph like this:

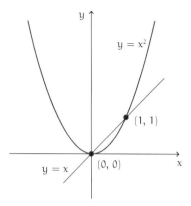

Intersections of $y = x^2$ and $y = x$

More Problems

"You learn by doing, not by thinking about doing."

In this section are some additional, slightly different problems for those who want to think more about the topics discussed in this book. The answers won't be given here, and there won't necessarily be only one correct solution.

I hope you'll take your time and enjoy these problems, either alone or with a friend.

Extra Chapter 1 Problems

Problem 1-X1 (Identities as figures)

Represent the following identity on a and b as a figure like that on page 9.

$$(a + b)^2 = a^2 + 2ab + b^2$$

Problem 1-X2 (Expansions)

Compare the expansion of $(a + b)^2$ with the expansion of $(a + b)^3$. Compare those with the expansion of $(a + b)^4$. Can you learn something from the comparison?

Problem 1-X3 (Sums and differences)

The conversation on page 8 discusses how it is much easier to calculate $10000 - 4$ than it is to calculate 102×98. But why is that? Will subtraction always be easier than multiplication? Just what makes for a simple calculation?

Problem 1-X4 (Inequalities)

On page 12, why does the narrator say the graph assumes that $a > b$? Also, what happens when $a = b$?

EXTRA CHAPTER 2 PROBLEMS

Problem 2-X1 (Systems of equations)

See what you can learn about the following system of equations:

$$\begin{cases} x + y & = 5 \\ 2x + 2y & = 10 \end{cases}$$

Problem 2-X2 (Systems of equations)

See what you can learn about the following system of equations:

$$\begin{cases} x + y & = 5 \\ 2x + 2y & = 9 \end{cases}$$

Problem 2-X3 (Systems of equations)

See what you can learn about the following system of equations:

$$\begin{cases} ax + by & = u \\ cx + dy & = v \end{cases}$$

EXTRA CHAPTER 3 PROBLEMS

Problem 3-X1 (Writing polynomials)

Miruka says that we write polynomials the way we do to make it easier to compare them and so that we can quickly verify their degree (see page 43). What do you think about that? Do you have anything to add about writing polynomials?

Problem 3-X2 (Ordering powers)

One of the rules for writing polynomials (see page 43) is that their terms should be sorted into order of decreasing power. Can you think of a reason why it might be better to write the terms in ascending order instead?

Problem 3-X3 (Graphing)

Draw the graph of $y = (x+1)^2 - 1$. Compare that to the graph of $y = (x-1)^2 - 1$. Compare those to the graph of $y = (x-100)^2 - 1$.

Problem 3-X4 (Graphing)

Draw the graph of $x = y^2 - 1$. Compare that graph to the graph of $y = x^2 - 1$.

Problem 3-X5 (Graphing)

Can you draw the graph of $y = x^{100}$? What do you think that graph would look like? How would it compare to the graph of $y = x^{99}$?

EXTRA CHAPTER 4 PROBLEMS

Problem 4-X1 (Reading graphs)

Look for a line graph in a newspaper, etc. What can you read from its shape?

Problem 4-X2 (Drawing graphs)

Draw the graph of $y = x + \dfrac{1}{x}$.

Problem 4-X3 (Playing with axes)

Draw the graph of $y = x^2$, but instead of an x-axis, use an x^2-axis.

Problem 4-X4 (Playing with axes)

Draw the graph of $y = \dfrac{1}{x}$, but instead of an x-axis, use a $\dfrac{1}{x}$ axis.

Problem 4-X5 (The names of things)

Why are parabolas called parabolas? Why are hyperbolas called hyperbolas?

EXTRA CHAPTER 5 PROBLEMS

Problem 5-X1 (Intersections of parabolas)

Find the intersection of the parabolas $y = -x^2 + 1$ and $y = x^2 - 1$.

Problem 5-X2 (The meaning of $y = 0$)

In a two-dimensional coordinate plane, the x-axis can be represented by the equation $y = 0$. What is $y = 0$ in a *three-dimensional* coordinate space?

Problem 5-X3 (Tangents)

The indicated points in the graphs on the left are considered tangents, but those in the graphs on the right are not. Can you describe the difference between the two?

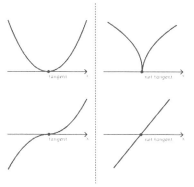

Appendix: Greek Letters

Lowercase	Uppercase	Name
α	A	alpha
β	B	beta
γ	Γ	gamma
δ	Δ	delta
ϵ ε	E	epsilon
ζ	Z	zeta
η	H	eta
θ ϑ	Θ	theta
ι	I	iota
κ ϰ	K	kappa
λ	Λ	lambda
μ	M	mu
ν	N	nu
ξ	Ξ	xi
o	O	omicron
π ϖ	Π	pi
ρ	P	rho
σ	Σ	sigma
τ	T	tau
υ	Υ	upsilon
φ φ	Φ	phi
χ	X	chi
ψ	Ψ	psi
ω	Ω	omega

Afterword

Thank you for reading this book, a collection of "math talk" conversations between Tetra, Miruka, Yuri, and of course the narrator. I hope you enjoyed it.

I would like to close with a word about how this book came to be.

I've been writing the *Math Girls* series of "mathematical teen romance" novels since 2007. Those books cover topics from many areas of mathematics, and quite a few readers have told me that they had to skip some of the harder bits.

In 2012, I began publishing a series of stories called "Math Girls: Secret Notebooks" on the website *Cakes*, which were conversations between the characters from the *Math Girls* books focusing on simpler mathematical topics. This book is a rearrangement of the first ten conversations in that series.

As with the *Math Girls* series, this book was produced using LaTeX 2_ε and the AMS Euler font. I would like to thank Haruhiko Okumura for his book *Introduction to Creating Beautiful Documents with LaTeX 2_ε*, which was an invaluable aid during layout. I created the graphs for the original Japanese edition using Microsoft Visio, Gnuplot, and the elementary mathematics handout macro *emath* by Kazuhiro Okuma (a.k.a. tDB), for which I am very grateful.

I would also like to thank the following persons for proofreading my drafts and giving me invaluable feedback, as well as those who did so anonymously. Of course, any errors remaining in the book are solely the responsibility of the author.

Ryo Akazawa, Yuta Asami, Tatsuya Igarashi, Tetsuya Ishiu, Ryuta Ishimoto, Kazuhiro Inaba, Ryuhei Uehara, Daiki Kawakami, Midori Kawakami, Iwao Kimura, Jun Kudo, Kazuhiro Kezuka, Kayo Kotaki, Akiko Sakaguchi, Naoki Norimatsu, Hiroaki Hanada, Aya Hayashi, Yutori Bonten (Medaka College), Masahide Maehara, Nami Masuda, Kiyoshi Miyake, Ken Murai, Yusuke Muraoka, Kenta Murata (mrkn), Tsutomu Yano, Kenji Yamaguchi

I would like to thank my editor at Softbank Creative, Kimio Nozawa, for his continuous support throughout the entire *Math Girls* series; I hope he sticks with me for this one, as well.

I thank Sadaaki Kato, of Cakes.

I thank all my readers for the support they've given my writing.

I thank my dearest wife and our two sons.

And I thank you, for having read this far. I hope to see you again in the next book.

Hiroshi Yuki

June, 2013

http://www.hyuki.com/girl/

Index

Other works by Hiroshi Yuki

(in English)

- *Math Girls*, Bento Books, 2011
- *Math Girls 2: Fermat's Last Theorem*, Bento Books, 2012
- *Math Girls Manga*, Bento Books, 2013

(in Japanese)

- *The Essence of C Programming*, Softbank, 1993 (revised 1996)
- *C Programming Lessons, Introduction*, Softbank, 1994 (Second edition, 1998)
- *C Programming Lessons, Grammar*, Softbank, 1995
- *An Introduction to CGI with Perl, Basics*, Softbank Publishing, 1998
- *An Introduction to CGI with Perl, Applications*, Softbank Publishing, 1998
- *Java Programming Lessons (Vols. I & II)*, Softbank Publishing, 1999 (revised 2003)

- *Perl Programming Lessons, Basics*, Softbank Publishing, 2001

- *Learning Design Patterns with Java*, Softbank Publishing, 2001 (revised and expanded, 2004)

- *Learning Design Patterns with Java, Multithreading Edition*, Softbank Publishing, 2002

- *Hiroshi Yuki's Perl Quizzes*, Softbank Publishing, 2002

- *Introduction to Cryptography Technology*, Softbank Publishing, 2003

- *Hiroshi Yuki's Introduction to Wikis*, Impress, 2004

- *Math for Programmers*, Softbank Publishing, 2005

- *Java Programming Lessons, Revised and Expanded (Vols. I & II)*, Softbank Creative, 2005

- *Learning Design Patterns with Java, Multithreading Edition, Revised Second Edition*, Softbank Creative, 2006

- *Revised C Programming Lessons, Introduction*, Softbank Creative, 2006

- *Revised C Programming Lessons, Grammar*, Softbank Creative, 2006

- *Revised Perl Programming Lessons, Basics*, Softbank Creative, 2006

- *Introduction to Refactoring with Java*, Softbank Creative, 2007

- *Math Girls / Fermat's Last Theorem*, Softbank Creative, 2008

- *Revised Introduction to Cryptography Technology*, Softbank Creative, 2008

- *Math Girls Comic (Vols. I & II)*, Media Factory, 2009

- *Math Girls / Gödel's Incompleteness Theorems*, Softbank Creative, 2009

- *Math Girls / Randomized Algorithms*, Softbank Creative, 2011

- *Math Girls / Galois Theory*, Softbank Creative, 2012

- *Java Programming Lessons, Third Edition (Vols. I & II)*, Softbank Creative, 2012

- *Etiquette in Writing Mathematical Statements: Fundamentals*, Chikuma Shobo, 2013

- *Math Girls Secret Notebook / Equations & Graphs*, Softbank Creative, 2013

- *Math Girls Secret Notebook / Let's Play with the Integers*, Softbank Creative, 2013

- *The Birth of Math Girls,* Softbank Creative, 2013

Made in the USA
Columbia, SC
19 May 2019